Everything I Needed To Know About Saving The World I Learned Before I Was Ten

A Manual For Human Survival

By

Craigy Franklin
(The child)

and

Gary Hutchison PhD
(The grown-up)
[Well, sort of!]

EVERYTHING I NEEDED TO KNOW ABOUT SAVING THE WORLD I LEARNED BEFORE I WAS TEN, is an original publication of *The Family of Man Press*.

The Family of Man Press
A division of G. F. Hutchison Press
310 South Block Avenue, Suite 17
Fayetteville, AR 72701

Copyright © 2002, 2005 by Gary F Hutchison
ISBN: 1-885631-56-1

All rights reserved, which includes the right to reproduce this book or portion thereof in any form whatsoever except as provided by the U S Copyright Law.

Printed in USA

PR 10 9 8 7 6 5 4 3 2

Dedication

To those wise men, women, and children
who, within every generation,
rediscover the secrets for
saving the world,
and
To those who are wise enough to listen
and implement those ideas
in their daily lives.

-- GFH

TABLE OF CONTENTS

Forward	9
An Explanation	11
Section One: Craigy Sets Out To Save The World	15
Section Two: Early Impressions of My Fellow Man (and more that a few suggestions for God!)	27
Section Three: Twenty-four Positive Agreements	51
Topic one: Basing one's life on love	51
Topic two: Love must be guided	56
Topic three: Making man's survival paramount	59
Topic four: Basis for judging self-worth	63
Topic five: Basing life on positive values	71
Topic six: Regularly modeling one's values	74
Topic seven: Emphasizing cooperation	77
Topic eight: Maintaining an altruistic focus	80
Topic nine: Making the first move	84
Topic ten: Maintaining a sense of humor	87
Topic eleven: The Positive Social Encounter	91
Topic twelve: Importance of modeling values	93
Topic thirteen: Honesty, tact and integrity	95
Topic fourteen: Focus on behavior not person	99
Topic fifteen: Understanding *their* meaning	102
Topic sixteen: Use of specific terms	106
Topic seventeen: Cautions about categories	108
Topic eighteen: Focusing on solutions	110
Topic nineteen: Acting only on verifiable facts	114
Topic twenty: Respecting possessions	119
Topic twenty one: Taking car of oneself	122
Topic twenty two: Remaining curious about people	126
Topic twenty three: Openness to differing beliefs	130
Topic twenty four: Accepting the unknown	133
Appendix One: The Johnny Appleseed of Smiles	139
Appendix Two: Building a User-friendly Society	147
Additional Books from The Family of Man Press	155

FORWARD

I hate *Forwards*! I've always hated *Forwards*. I hate to read *Forwards*. I hate to write *Forwards*. They delay one from getting to the meat of the book (apologies to my vegetarian readers). They (forwards, not vegetarians) seem to imply that either the author feels he has to justify what he has written or he believes the reader is so dull-witted as to need some before-the-fact explanation about what will follow. By its mere name – *Forward* – it further implies that it comes before the book, which is clearly not the case since it resides within the covers. (Thanks for listening. I feel much better, now!)
"So," **I** said to **my**self, "I'll be more enlightened and write a *Preface,* instead." I took out Mr. Webster just to make sure. It read, *"Preface – to be preliminary to; a Forward."* Devastated that Old Dan had failed me, I dumped the whole Forward idea. ("So," **you** say to **your**self, "How can it be, then, that I am reading it?" Perhaps in the next edition, I will include a Preface to the Forward, which will explain all that.)
Being an honest sort - which I hope will become clear as you read on – I have, on the following page, substituted the more accurate and descriptive heading for what I need to accomplish here at the outset.

AN EXPLANATION OF THINGS IMPLIED ALL QUITE ESOTERICALLY BY THE AUTHOR WHO WOULD RATHER ADD A STATEMENT UP FRONT THAN MAKE THE MORE APPROPRIATE, EFFORT-FILLED, MODIFICATIONS WHERE THEY BELONG WITHIN THE TEXT PROPER

I entered the World with an extra-large portion of intellectual horsepower (a nebulous term but one generally understood to imply great ease of learning, abstracting and remembering). I take no credit for that and only mention it here so the reader will understand how, at such an early age, I was able to generalize from what I observed in those around me to the axioms of 'world saving' social values and behaviors that prompted this volume. It also accounts for my rapid progression through school. The best accommodation it could make to my unusual situation was to double promote me each year – I spent one semester in each grade.

At nine, unhampered by things such as years of relevant experience, the careful study of man's accumulated knowledge, and personally acquired wisdom, saving the World (*mankind*, really) seemed a pretty straight forward, simple, operation to me.

Recently, as I reviewed the diaries that I had kept between ages six and ten (over 1,600 pages), it all rushed back at me. Once again (55 years later) it seems all quite straightforward and simple. What goes haywire between ten and sixty-five? (That is not a rhetorical question, but one that *will* go unanswered for the time being.)

The diary entries, which are used here to illustrate the child's take on the topics, are presented pretty much as they were written. Sometimes passages from several entries have been combined to facilitate the flow of thoughts. I have doctored (pun intended – get used to them!) the punctuation here and there to make passages more readable (adding quotation marks, for example). Portions of entries that didn't relate to the topic have typically been omitted (unless they're just so darn cute I couldn't resist including them!). Omissions are indicated by dots . . . . The parentheses here ( ) were all in the originals. Brackets [ ] contain explanatory information [or inane comments] I added, during editing, often as much for my own enjoyment as the reader's enlightenment. I have also included, in brackets, the grade I was in at the time of each entry to help keep the interplay between grade and age in perspective [age and grade replace the dates which were in the original diary].

It may be useful to note that as a youngster, in the privacy of my diary, I could play with precise, *"quarter"* words and language, rather than the more commonplace, *"penny"* and *"nickel"* words, which I found more acceptable as I went about my day to day interaction with the residents of Springtown. During editing, I toyed with the idea of dummying up that vocabulary here, to make it more age-level-believable, but in the end left it as it had been originally set down. (The reader may double Craigy's age and then subtract one year to get a rough approximation of his vocabulary age at any point – age 7½ times two less one would approach 14.)

Folks are often bewildered by my several names so let me attempt a concise clarification. When, after my parents died and I was taken as a toddler into the home of Fred and Wilma Franklin, they had me use their last name to provide a sense of family unity. I also went by the nickname, Craigy, since it was a favorite name of theirs. When I was seventeen, after they had both passed away, I began using my birth name, Gary Hutchison.

In my Diary, I often wrote to it as if it were another Being. Somewhere along the line, I shortened *Dear Diary* to *Dear Di* and eventually to just *Di*. Let Craigy explain in his own words.

AGE 7 ½ [Grade five]
DEAR DI,
 I REALLY LIKE WRITING TO YOU - OR SHOULD THAT BE IN YOU OR ON YOU - IF YOU WERE A SHEEP IT WOULD CLEARLY BE ON EWE! HA! HA!
 I THINK OF YOU AS MY BEST FRIEND AFTER GINNY. I

KNOW YOU AREN'T REALLY ALIVE BUT I THINK EVERY TIME I WRITE IN YOU, YOU ABSORB A PART OF ME, SO IN THAT WAY, YOU'RE BECOMING MORE AND MORE ALIVE EVERY DAY. (I FEEL LIKE THE GEPPETTO OF DIARIES!!!)
    WHEN I'M WRITING IN YOU IT'S OFTEN LIKE YOU WON'T LET ME GET BY WITH AN INCOMPLETE OR POORLY CONSTRUCTED IDEA. ONCE IT'S DOWN ON A PAGE, YOU SEEM TO URGE ME ON TO 'FIX' IT OR COMPLETE IT OR SOMETIMES EVEN SCRAP IT ENTIRELY. THANKS FOR THAT. I KNOW I'M NOT EASY TO SWAY ONCE I GET SOMETHING IN MY HEAD.
    WE'VE BEEN AT THIS SINCE BEFORE I WAS FOUR, BACK WHEN MOM WROTE IN YOU FOR ME. I GUESS THAT MAKES YOU ABOUT 3 ½ BY NOW. WHEN I READ OVER WHAT YOU HAVE TO SAY, YOU SEEM PRETTY SMART. YOU ALWAYS UNDERSTAND ME, AND YOU NEVER JUDGE ME HARSHER THAN I JUDGE MYSELF. I LOVE YOUR SENSE OF HUMOR AND YOU KNOW WHAT ELSE, DI? IF ANYBODY ELSE EVER READ THIS PAGE THEY'D SEND ME TO THE LOONY BIN - DO NOT PASS GO; DO NOT COLLECT $100; PROCEED DIRECTLY TO THE LOONY BIN. PERHAPS I SHOULD STOP. JUST ONE MORE THING, DI - I TRULY DO LOVE AND CHERISH THE RELATIONSHIP WE HAVE.
    YOUR BEST FRIEND,
    CRAIGY

One final consideration here: Are the ideas and insights expressed in Craigy's diaries truly his? He talked with Di about that when he was nine and seemed to understand his situation.

AGE 9 [grade 8]
    DEAR DI,
    ... I'VE DECIDED IT'S DIFFICULT TO KNOW WHICH OF MY DISCOVERIES ABOUT LIFE ARE ACTUAL DISCOVERIES OF MINE AND WHICH ARE THINGS I'VE READ AND HEARD. I KNOW THAT EVEN WHEN IT IS SOMETHING I HAVE DISCOVERED ON <u>MY</u> OWN, THAT DOESN'T MEAN

THAT SOMEBODY ELSE HASN'T ALSO DISCOVERED IT ON THEIR OWN.

I LOVE BEING A HUMAN BEING! BEYOND HAVING AN OPPOSABLE THUMB AND LANGUAGE, WE PEOPLE ARE SO WONDERFULLY VERSATILE. FOR EXAMPLE, IF I WERE A TREE, I COULD NEVER GO OUT ON A LIMB ABOUT ONE OF MY IDEAS. IF I WERE A FLOWER, I COULD NEVER BLOSSOM INTO A CARING PARENT. IF I WERE A STONE, I'D NEVER GET TO ROCK MY KIDS TO SLEEP AT NIGHT. (THIS IS GREAT, ISN'T IT, DI?) IF I WERE A MATTRESS, I WOULD NEVER BE PRONE TO SPRING TO LIFE OVER A NEW IDEA (I'D PROBABLY JUST SLEEP ON IT!!) IF I WERE A CLOCK, MY FACE COULD NEVER INDICATE WHAT A GREAT TIME I WAS HAVING. (YOU HAVE TO 'HAND' IT TO ME - THAT WAS CLEVER!) IF I WERE A WHEEL, I COULD NEVER GET TIRED. (WAIT! PERHAPS I SPOKE TOO SOON. NOT GETTING TIRED MIGHT NOT BE SO BAD. LET ME GET MY BEARINGS ON THAT BEFORE I ROLL ON.) . . .

The passage clearly deteriorates over the next eight, pun punctuated, pages. One thing about Craigy, he never let a little thing like failure keep him from trying – and believe me, many adults in Springtown thought Craigy was VERY trying! Craigy had a heart as big as all outdoors but was dauntless once he took up a cause.

I hope what follows will be insightful and useful, but if not insightful and useful, at least a lot of fun!

- Gary Hutchison

SECTION ONE

Craigy Sets Out To Save The World

Prior to the time in my young life when my being became absorbed with such all-consuming concerns as hair, pimples, social status and – the most thoroughly distracting and confusing of all – girls, I spent considerable time observing and reflecting on the human condition. Between six and ten I made numerous discoveries and arrived at a number of principles (agreements) which I was convinced would solve all of man's ills and produce a veritable paradise on Earth.

Since I was endowed with a great deal more cerebral proficiency than was in any way reasonable, I was indeed fortunate to have adults in my life that always listened with interest and support to my questions, concerns, ideas and hypotheses. I was, therefore, quite certain that all I needed to do was present my miraculous findings to them and in a matter of weeks (a month at the most) my principles would be implemented worldwide and life would become simply grand for everyone. There would be no bullies, no wars, no poverty or hunger. People would live happily in safety, leading productive, personally meaningful lives, based on love, demonstrating a willing and eager, mutual helpfulness.

With such a major contribution accomplished prior to my tenth birthday, I had some all quite serious concerns about just how

I would productively occupy the remaining eight or nine decades of my life.

It was at age nine that I first encountered the most pernicious of all intellectual monsters - the *"Yesbutt"* (the final 't' was added for reasons – not entirely pure of heart - that will become clear). I would present my list of principles to adult after adult (those outside my immediate, supportive circle). They would listen (well, most would listen. I guess I had a reputation of being doggedly tenacious even at an early age so they knew it was best to just let Craigy get it off his chest). They would nod. (I would take that to be encouraging.) When I finished, the lurking monster (all that time quietly, invisibly, skulking in the shadows of their minds) would inevitably rear its head. *"Yes but . . ."* They would proceed to agree that, *yes*, if enacted my principles would in fact save the World, *but* then would proceed to tell me why they could never be enacted.

"They work in my home," I'd rebut.

"*Yes but* that's a special situation," they would come back.

"All the adults I've talked with about my plan agree it is a good one."

"*Yes but* even good plans often don't work."

"The plan is flawlessly logical."

"*Yes but* most people don't act logically."

"My plan meets all of man's positive emotional and physical needs."

"*Yes but*! *Yesbut! Yesbutt . . . !*"

It came to me that I had virtually never encountered a "yes but" emanating from anyone ages ten and under. I proceeded up the age scale to determine when it surfaced. Perhaps it was related to hormones. Perhaps it was a virus to which kids - up to some certain age - had a natural immunity.

The biggest *Yesbutts* were definitely between the ages of thirty and sixty. Once I began tapping the 65+ age group, I noticed a definite mellowing. Even those who had been the most dyed in the wool Yesbutts prior to retirement, rapidly grew into the more comfortable and helpful *Givitagoers*.

Thus came about my four categories of responders to ideas

for social change.

There were the *Letsdoiters* who were generally under age eleven, although forty-two year old Miss Oakley – she was known to wear slacks and buy instant coffee, so most of the women of the town looked down on her – somehow seemed to have escaped catching the Yesbutt syndrome. I loved to talk with her. No topic was ever off limits and no idea was ever rejected out of hand as unworthy. I wished she had been a teacher – goodness knows, we needed more teachers with those traits. But I digress. (One of the traits I have always admired most in myself!)

People from eleven into their mid to late twenties were the *Disticks* (Disinterested Skeptics). They'd neither offer discouragement nor encouragement – they just didn't seem to have the time or energy necessary to contemplate events occurring outside their own heads. (I assigned the blame for this in males to the rampant growth of ugly hair over the private areas of their bodies and to the female's eventual insistence on wearing sweaters and blouses having those two unsightly bumps in them!)

Those falling within the thirty to sixty or sixty-five age range were the aforementioned *Yesbutts,* who always had long lists of reasons why new ideas would not – could not – work, and therefore should not be tried. I figured they were probably terrified at having their lives turned upside down, so they went out of their way to prove the worth of the status quo or at least protect it from all boat-rockers. (Look in the dictionary under *boat-rocker* to see a picture of Craigy Franklin at age nine!)

Then, the *Givitagoers,* those past retirement age, seemed to project some mixture of what had been, what was, and what might have been. It was a kind of wisdom that *allowed for possibilities* other than those they had lived and known, and in most instances, had even treasured.

So, early on, several unexpected stumbling blocks loomed in my campaign to save the world. Unfortunately, the nay-sayers – primarily the Yesbutts – seemed to hold the power in my world.

Those with kindred spirits were either too young to effect change (the Letsdoiters) or too old and feeble to provide any muscle (the Givitagoers) - though both groups were long on encouragement, and I appreciated that.

Pop had what seemed to be a modestly helpfully suggestion: Encourage the Givitagoers and the Letsdoiters to demonstrate, in the way they live, just how helpful and powerful my principles really were. It was the best advice I have ever been given, although I didn't fully understand that at nine.

Eventually, I came to see that when you tried to push ideas on someone else they typically reacted by needing to defensively prove their own way was better or right. An attack on their way of living was an attack on the core of their self-concept and only one's life itself is typically more tenaciously defended than one's ego.

Discussions with them, therefore, were really not *discussions* at all. I would state one of my principles and say they should adopt it. While I was building my case, they were not really listening, but instead using that time to think up counter arguments that would support their previous – comfortable – position. In that way, they really never heard the details of my position that they were so tenaciously arguing against.

The *Yesbutt Generation* was clearly the worst about using this defensive positioning rather than listening. Interesting to me, they thought it was a fine approach when *they* utilized it, but they became enraged when *their teenagers* used the same strategy with them (and teenagers ALWAYS do, of course!).

I thought long and hard about Pop's advice. It made sense. I realized that when I admired the way a person lived or what he had accomplished in life, I tended to emulate him. Part of my problem was contained in the concept *'admire'*. It was inextricably tied to what one believed was the most important goal in life – the purpose for living. Bullies were admired by those whose purpose was acquiring personal power. Teachers by those valuing knowledge. The clerics, when spiritual aspects were held in highest esteem. The Yesbutts when it was the status quo one sought to preserve. The rich and famous for those who sought status and personal worth in such artificial accomplishments, fully divorced (I thought) from the true purpose of living - being a helpful person.

My most basic problem, then, was how to convince people to cooperatively strive for a World in which the universal human condition was positive, and where love, compassion, reciprocal esteem, and mutual facilitation were the means for achieving and maintaining it.

It appeared to me that the Yesbutt Generation – in particular – was so deeply committed to accumulating great piles of stuff or power to prove themselves worthy (successful), that they had little room left in their beings to consider that *stuff* was relatively meaningless compared with assisting one's fellow-men. It was black and white to me – abject selfishness vs. necessary altruism. The stockpilers vs. the sharers. Those who thought in terms of ME vs. those who thought in terms of US.

When I curled up in bed at night and thought back over my day, it was always the nice and helpful things I'd been able to do for others that filled my young being with feelings of contentment and self-worth. In a passage from my diary at age fifteen, I referred to that feeling (somewhat indelicately, perhaps, though from the perspective of a fifteen year old male it represented the ultimate height of positive feelings) as "the orgasm of inner joy." Later, in my books about the *Little People of the Ozark Mountains*™ I coined the word *'fuzzalatious'* to cover the same set of wonder-filled, deep down inside, warm, feelings. At nine, I had no catchy phrase – perhaps that would have helped my cause – so herein I may from time to time borrow from the Little People's vocabulary in order to proceed with an economy of words.

Since my call to arms based on logic had been relatively unsuccessful, I decided to go the route of common sense. Although it seemed blatantly clear to me that logic and common sense were cut form the same cloth, most others, interestingly, did not make that connection. 'Logic', I came to understand, was the less trusted, Ivory Tower version of the *If this - Then that* connection, while 'common sense' was the dependable, reliable, *if-then* connection of the common man. "*If* treating people in one way curtailed crime (for example), *then* it was only *common sense* to treat them that way." Call that common sense and it was immediately accepted. Call it logical and it produced immediate skepticism.

Armed with my new, more laid back, less academic approach, I went forth to again make my attempt at saving the world. But again, the army of Yesbutts remained steadfast. In fact, I noted a substantial increase in their defensive maneuvering. That told me (at ten) one thing for sure. Common sense (in which they tended to believe) was even more threatening to them than logic. One principle of human behavior became clear: 'The more powerful (believable, perhaps) the threatening belief, the more resistance a person manifests.' (Stated another way: 'The more reasonable the threatening information, the more resistance the person manifests – up to a point.' It is usually *that* point at which either the teen or the parent marches out of the room, the one with the most clearly reasonable argument remaining victoriously behind.)

I'd seen it in Harold, a fifteen year old who was particularly kind to me and who would come over and play catch or shoot baskets with me. There were times when his parents got on him unmercifully about something he had done - something that he really could have cared less about ever doing again. But, the reasonableness implicit in their reaction seemed to force him to defend what he had done and turned it into something he just needed to keep doing.

I climbed the huge pear tree behind our house to reconnoiter. I was dumbfounded (as a youthful pacifist) when I recognized that both logic and common sense were tantamount to using force when it came to trying to change another's behavior (at least among the Yesbutts and their teenagers.).

If the lessons of history and the discoveries of psychology had demonstrated anything, it was that force and punishment were the least effective (almost always ineffective, in fact) means for making long-term changes in behavior. Long term change only came through personal commitment to some belief or value or goal, and personal commitment seemed to evolve most readily when someone witnessed a meaningfully dramatic demonstration of the merit (power), which the belief, value, or goal held.

So, it was back to Pop's wise observation that *effective model-*

ling was at the core of initiating positive change (or negative change, also, for that matter).

It brought me back to thinking about the importance of what a person holds as his most important personal concern or goal. That seemed to be the bedrock, the ultimate starting point. My plan would be to go out of my way to become an altruistic model for those folks whose main goal in life was to be rich, or to own a big house, or fancy car, or to achieve great power. It seemed a less difficult task to sell my ideas to those folks whose ultimate concerns were things like improved mental health, housing for the poor, or a healthy planet.

What had initially seemed a simple sell had quickly become an extremely complex undertaking. I needed to beat a strategic retreat and regroup. I needed to find some common ground upon which I could approach the fully selfish folks on the one hand and the altruistic on the other, while accommodating everybody in between.

Three pears later, the flickering of an idea occurred to me. "Happy, productive, helpful, well-adjusted people (four of my plan's basic goals) were clearly both easier to live with *and* less of a financial burden to society as a whole than their opposites." The altruists would certainly understand the importance of that statement if only out of compassion for their fellow man. I figured that even the most self-centered, cold-blooded, hard-hearted person on Earth would also buy into the idea, because it meant in the long run he would have to spend less tax money for social programs (mental health, crime, poverty) and was more likely to be able to live in a more comfortable, safe, crime-free, neighborhood.

I tried it out on Mom and Pop first. After a thorough discussion (with actual, mutual listening involved), they agreed it fit both ends of the continuum I had set up (altruistic and self-centered). I took the idea on the road. First to Doc. He agreed with very little discussion, and although he didn't discourage me, I could tell he believed my plan was doomed to failure. I admired Doc a great deal – after Mom and Pop, probably more than anyone I knew – but he and I had disagreed about man's basic human nature my whole life (well, for the six years of it that I could remember, at least). He saw man's nature as dark. I saw it as positively constructive. He thought the bad stuff was buried deep and immutably in man's genes. I believed that dark side only flourished when a child failed to learn positive values such as compassion, helpfulness, and self-respect based on integrity. (I was, as you can imagine, some bothered that such a wise man as Doc held a totally different point of view from mine, but I would live with that until life proved one of us right.)

In fact, Doc had once said he hoped I was right about man's nature and would prove him wrong. That suddenly seemed to put the weight of the world on my young shoulders. (It is that overwhelming burden that I detail in another autobiographical book, *36 Hours to Live*.)

My discussion with Parson went on and on, but really never addressed the main issue. He got off onto the idea that people who would go along with my plan just so they could live a safer, more comfortable life among more congenial people, were *doomed-to-hell-sinners*. He went on and on about how it was the "intention' not the action or outcome that had to be pure and Godly. I listened but probably not with a completely open mind after the first half-hour. I was late for a ball game at John's, which meant I'd be stuck out in left field again.

The discussion quickly petered out when I asked him, "If all you have said about intention is true, then how is it you accept Harry Osco's donations to the church when everyone knows he is all quite intentionally the most ungodly man who's ever trod the streets of our little town?"

(I walked three times, got one hit, and caught one of the six fly balls that came my way in left field, so I was a pretty happy nine year-old by supper time.)

That summer I pursued the field of psychology and read everything that I could find on the subject. I was pleased to learn that John Watson and B. F. Skinner had proved the importance of positive reinforcement in changing behavior – something I had personally discovered sometime prior to my 6th birthday. I was more taken, however, by the field of Phenomenology. It showed that people act on what they 'believe' is real, rather than on what may 'actually' be real. In fact, in terms of human behavior, 'real reality' virtually never plays any significant role. (If we think a guy is dangerous, we react to him as if he were dangerous, even though in "reality" he's a safe, saintly person.)

All of that, coupled with the gnawing realization (thanks to Parson) that to know a man's heart you needed to know his intentions not just his deeds – provided new dimensions for me to explore and utilize in fulfilling my life's mission.

Regardless of all the new things I learned, it all kept coming back to *modeling*. *Show* people the benefits of living a compassionate, helpful, love-based life and they just might try it themselves. Modeling seemed to initiate a whole lot less defensiveness in folks than did discussions, logic and common sense. Still, I could see that a little kid's actions were seldom taken very seriously (as a model of behavior for adults). A nice, well behaved, helpful, little kid (which I was) got lots of smiles and unending pats on the head (perhaps that explained why I remained so short) but I doubted he was looked upon as a model for adults' behavior. Although I hated to have my hair ruffled, I had to admit the experience reinforced my belief in my mission – my values.

The light bulb lit brightly above my head. *That* was the secret. It all fell into place early one morning as I was looking down from my favorite oak tree, watching the first beams of daylight chase the shadows across the graves of my biological parents. Use Skinner's reinforcement techniques to establish universally applicable *basic positive values* (intentions) rather than merely building situation-specific *behaviors* (deeds).

That suggested that one would not have rules for kids based on what they could and couldn't *do* (behaviors), but rather guidelines that would help them make decisions about their own behaviors based on their *positive values*. (Had my **W**isdom **Q**uotient matched my 165+ **I**ntelligence **Q**uotient, I would have realized *that* was essentially the way Mom and Pop had raised me – even without ever having read Skinner, Watson, Freud, Snygg, Combs, James, or Craigy Franklin. Modeling! Reinforcing *values*! It just doesn't get much more positively powerful than that!)

So, I would enlist a band of folks to model behaviors based on positive values that would encourage others to accept those underlying values and use them to guide their own behaviors so the human condition would be forever improved. It worked fine right up to that last phrase. Someway, *improving the human condition* had to become each person's ultimate incentive, and quite clearly that was *not* the case.

Well, it *was* the case for altruists – about ten percent of the population according to my experiences (Doc put it at more like two percent.). The rest seemed more concerned (except on Sunday morning, perhaps) about improving *their own* condition. They rationalized their position by saying, "I take care of myself so, others can (should) take care of themselves."

It was akin to the big lie promoted by motivational speakers: "You can be anything you want to be." I wanted to be just an average kid, a little taller and a lot dumber – that could never happen. Perry, a mentally retarded friend of mine wanted to be an airline pilot – that could never be. We all have limitations – sometimes fewer than we believe, I'll admit - but to deny their limit-setting power is a giant deception.

[Excuse another digression but it really felt good, so just be happy for me!]

As the phenomenologists pointed out, people invent a perception of reality that reinforces their own needs or biases. If I believe that since I can take care of myself, that indicates that everybody else can do the same – my version of reality - then I am relieved of any responsibility for them or their welfare or even for the future, human generations. (It may be a perception – like the one above – that is based in ignorance, but the quality of its source becomes irrelevant once it becomes one's reality.)

My basic job, as it turned out, was to find ways of helping people include in their definitions of reality the concept *that improving the human condition must be everybody's primary concern.* To do that, people had to become convinced just how *precious* the human being – the human species – was. There had to be locked links between emotion and logic, passion and values.

Once that was achieved, the rest would be easy. Clearly, certain ways of treating and approaching people and society improve things for everybody – other ways harm, even devastate things. I felt that certainly anyone with an IQ larger than his shoe size should be able to understand that!!!

Later, as I read man's history more seriously (as a teen), I was fascinated to realize that just as I had "discovered" the agreements necessary to establish and maintain a humanity-friendly social order, so had thinkers of *every* previous generation also discovered those same truths.

So, why had the World remained in such a mess? I think I found the answer in that tree when I was nine. It's not the rules of appropriate *behavior* that have been elusive. It is the unwavering commitment to the necessary *value-base* that seems missing – or at least floundering in a sea of nearsighted selfishness.

It seemed such a simple concept at ten. *"If every neighbor in the world would willingly and eagerly just make sure that the neighbors on each side of him were safe, well taken care of, happy, and had reasons to be self-respecting, then everyone in the world would live in a positive human condition – in a humanity-friendly environment."*

At sixty-five, it still seems a simple concept. Perhaps the details need to be specified. That runs against my grain. I've always believed in providing sound, broad, generalized, value-based principles that people could then *thoughtfully* apply to a wide range of situations and conditions (rather than trying to cover each possible, specific situation with a rule or law).

Perhaps by considering the two-dozen *Positive Social Agreements* (Section Three) that I believe people must make and keep with each other, folks will be able to work backwards and formulate that single, general principle, themselves.

I have divided Section Three into several dozen areas. Within each, I first state the nature of each topic, illustrate it by the simplistic though often profound observations taken from Craigy's childhood diaries, and then pull all of that into an "Agreement" followed by some "grown-up" observations and discussion as the spirit moves me.

The *Agreements* are just that: Pledges to act in certain ways *with* one another (a two-way street). I imagine that you will find little that is new to you here. It is my hope, however, that the presentation will provide some gentle, concrete, reminders about the truths that you and I have known from a young age, and of the crucial, immediate, necessity to spread them (model them) among those whose lives you have the privilege of touching.

Before getting down to those more formal, concrete, nitty-gritty, aspects, let me lead you on a short romp around the little town that provided my introduction to social order and introduce you to some of the folks that helped form my early impressions of mankind.

SECTION TWO:

Early Impressions of My Fellow Man
(And more than a few suggestions for God !)

I grew up in a very small town during the 1940's and early 50's. Springtown (pseudonyms are used for the names of towns, landmarks, and all the people involved, to protect the privacy and dignity of my precious early friends and teachers) wasn't so much a wide spot in the road as it was a narrow corridor, three blocks wide and eleven blocks long, flanking both sides of the well-maintained, gravel, County Highway 111. The year I was eight, the Main Street was paved and we suddenly felt quite cosmopolitan.

To the east, was a wide, deep gully, home to the proverbial babbling creek and spanned by a wood-timber railroad trestle. The western border was defined by a small rise - *the hill*, we called it. There were large, two-story houses there replete with garages and halls. At an early age, I observed that a house with one or more halls defined it as belonging to rich people. The more square feet of hall, the richer the owner. The houses of us poorer folks didn't waste room on halls – a much more clever and efficient design to my way of thinking. Please note that in my mind, the rich guys were "people" and the rest of us were 'folks' – a generally compassionate, helpful and good-humored lot to which I was proud and pleased to belong.

Mom washed and ironed for the people on the hill so I gained many valuable, first hand, experiences as I made pick-ups and deliveries for Mom with my wagon. In general, they had little inclination to chat and were pretty much all business. I was continually amazed because their houses didn't ever look lived in. I fantasized that they must have some subterranean rooms to which I was not privy. Their homes never smelled like fresh baked cookies or bread. When they were asked to donate time to some worthy cause, like painting the County Home or rebuilding Jake's barn after the fire, they typically offered money instead of help - a very sad state, I thought. Perhaps they were allergic to many of the good things in life – conversation, home made fun, helping one another, and enjoying their homes and neighbors. It was an observation that held more truth than I could possibly have known at seven.

Those people on the hill weren't unkind, mind you, they just seemed disconnected from most things that Mom, Pop, and I treasured about life. And so it was that at an early age I developed a sincere compassion for those less fortunate people over on the hill who had to muddle through life with lots of money.

It all really came home to me the Christmas I was eight. I decided I wanted to make a card for every family in town – 204 in all. I'd make 210 just in case any Hobos stopped under the railroad trestle on Christmas Eve.

I worked at odd jobs around the community in order to earn the money I would need for paper, envelopes and other supplies. I spent most evenings during November and early December working on them – each one created to be a perfect match for the person or family to which it would go.

I fretted for a time over how they should be signed – from all three of us Franklins, or just me. I didn't want to be selfish about it. Finally, I shared my dilemma with Mom and Pop. Pop said that although he and Mom would be proud and honored to have their names on my cards, they were *my* cards, my idea, my money and my time. They thought the cards should just bear my name. They made it seem just right and then I could move on.

Each card had a seasonal picture on the front and a holiday verse or message – tailor-made for each family – on the inside. My printing was large, so the messages were necessarily short and to the point.

Few projects in my life have given me the warm, wonderful (fuzzalatious) feeling in my heart that came my way that Christmas.

But that is all preliminary to my insightful experience that season. In my plan, I had allowed fifteen minutes for each delivery. I figured they'd invite me in, open the card, and oooo and aaaah for a maximum of sixty seconds. Then we'd sit and chat for another ten minutes – maybe downing a cup of cocoa – and I'd then be off to the next house. (Considering the substantial amount of cocoa I expected to consume, I also scheduled time for bathroom breaks.)

That's pretty much the way it went – until I got to "the hill." There were only 19 houses I classified as "Hill Houses." I had set aside two hours on each of three evenings to make my deliveries up there. From the time I rapped on the first door, until the moment I arrived back in my kitchen, less than one hour had elapsed and I had delivered all 19 cards.

Most hadn't even opened the envelopes in my presence. Only six had invited me inside and I got the idea that was mostly to keep from losing heat. They all did say thank you but they just wouldn't or couldn't stop at that. Some offered me quarters – one even a fifty cent piece. Several took a small gift from under the tree – removed the card and handed it to me.

I quickly surmised that if I had been at home, none of these people would have ventured there to present me with quarters, gifts or apples. It was all like some kind of pay-back or trade-off.

I refused each gift or offer of silver with a smile and a polite, "No thank you. I'm not here to get things. I'm just here to give you the card I made for you."

Then there would come a soon predictable period of dead silence which I would break by smiling again, wish them a Merry Christmas, and wave as I turned and left.

They had missed the point. They seemed unable to comprehend the point. I loved the people and folks in my town. They represented my whole world. They were important to me. Most of the flatland folks understood about my love and that love was a one way thing – I chose to love them and didn't expect anything in return. They respected that. The people on the hill, however, fully missed the point. I wondered how they could have lived so many years and learned so little about living and loving.

I decided it was because the Hill People were more into having and getting more and more stuff, and less into honoring the *human* part of their being.

It was early experiences like that one that led me to become fascinated by, if not preoccupied with, the observation and study of human beings (hereafter called 'people' as an all-inclusive term).

My first simplistic categorization of people divided us into just two groups – those with PFL's (people-focused lives), and SFL's (stuff-focused lives). Although experience soon taught me that no category truly characterized any one member accurately (and, in fact, often led to gross misjudgments, prejudice and despicable acts), used judiciously, this dichotomy had great predictive value. During my thirty-five plus years as a clinical psychologist, I found that to initially determine if a person leans more toward the PFL or the SFL orientation is helpful. It becomes a very good predictor of the amount of unrelenting turmoil, family problems and unhappiness a person tends to experience day by day. [The SFL's experience persistent problems and the PFL's far fewer, less intense and more short-term problems.]

But this is adult extrapolation from my early experiences and I shall try to avoid that from here on.

By the time I was eight and a half, I began finding that my *People Categorizing System* didn't account for many of the troublesome human characteristics I was beginning to encounter. Eventually, those new observations led to an expanded system. I defer to the following several entries in my early diaries.

AGE 7   3:30 pm   [grade 5]

WELL I'LL TELL YOU, DI, THIS HAS BEEN THE <u>GREATEST</u> DAY IN MY WHOLE LONG LIFE. MARY ANN - BEAUTIFUL MARY ANN - SAID SHE'D COME OVER TO MY PLACE AFTER SCHOOL AND WE COULD DO OUR HOMEWORK TOGETHER AND THEN PLAY OR SOMETHING. PLAY SOUNDS GOOD. I'M NOT SURE WHAT "OR SOMETHING" MIGHT BE BUT I GUESS I'LL FIND OUT. FIFTH GRADE GIRLS SEEM PRETTY WORLDLY AND THEY STICK TOGETHER IN THINGS - LIKE MOST OF THEM CAME TO 5TH GRADE THIS YEAR WEARING SWEATERS AND BLOUSES WITH BIG BUMPS IN THEM. I THINK THEY LOOK PRETTY SILLY. GOTTA GO. SHE'LL BE HERE ANY MINUTE.

8:00 PM

WELL, I'LL TELL YOU, DI, THIS HAS BEEN THE WORST DAY IN MY WHOLE LIFE. MARY ANN CAME OVER BUT I DON'T THINK SHE REALLY LIKES ME THAT MUCH. SHE WAS NICE WHILE WE WORKED ON ARITHMETIC BUT I SAW SHE WAS JUST COPYING MY WORK. I DIDN'T SAY ANYTHING BUT IT DIDN'T SEEM RIGHT. WHEN WE FINISHED (WHEN I FINISHED, REALLY) SHE LOOKED AT THE CLOCK AND SAID IT WAS LATE AND SHE HAD TO GO. I SAID, "WHAT ABOUT PLAYING OR SOMETHING?" SHE SAID I COULD KISS HER IF I HURRIED UP. I SAID, "WHY WOULD I WANT TO KISS YOU?" SHE ROLLED HER EYES AND LEFT WITHOUT EVEN THANKING MOM FOR THE COOKIES.

GIRLS ARE PRETTY HARD TO UNDERSTAND AND I'LL TELL YOU ONE MORE THING, DI, I SUSPECT IT HAS SOMETGHING TO DO WITH THOSE BUMPY SWEATERS. ANYWAY, SHE JUST USED ME. THE UNIVERSITY TRIED TO USE ME WHEN THEY USED TO SEND PSYCHOLOGIST INTERNS OUT TO PRACTICE TESTING ME. POP FINALLY

PUT A STOP TO THAT. I GUESS WHEN I AGREE TO BE USED ITS OKAY. I JUST FEEL BAD FOR PEOPLE WHO'D RATHER TAKE ADVANTAGE OF OTHER PEOPLE INSTEAD OF TRYING TO DO SOMETHING ON THEIR OWN - HOW WILL THEY EVER KNOW IF THEY CAN REALLY DO THINGS OR NOT? PEOPLE USERS ARE A SAD LOT. THEY STEAL A PART OF YOU AND THINK THAT'S ALL OKAY.

AGE 8 [GRADE 7]
DEAR DI: I JUST CAME BACK FROM VISITING OLD MRS STEPHENS NEXT DOOR. I CAN NEVER TELL IF SHE'S HAPPY OR SAD. OH, HER FACE ALWAYS LIGHTS UP WHEN I GO TO SEE HER BUT HER MOOD IS HARD TO JUDGE. MOSTLY SHE SITS, LISTENS TO THE RADIO AND ROCKS. PERSONALLY, ROCKING MAKES ME CAR SICK BUT NOT HER I GUESS. (HMM! MAYBE IT'S REALLY THAT RIDING IN A CAR MAKES ME ROCKER SICK. I'LL HAVE TO THINK ON THAT.)

I WAS THINKING, WHEN I WAS WITH HER TODAY, THAT SHE IS LIKE A 'NOTHING BEING' - I MEAN SHE NEVER DOES ANYTHING. SHE WON'T GO TO QUILTING AT THE CHURCH - BOTH MOM AND I HAVE URGED THAT. SHE'LL TALK TO FOLKS BUT NOT ABOUT ANYTHING MEANINGFUL -MOSTLY WHO DID WHAT WITH WHOM AND WHEN. SHE'S LIVED HERE IN SPRINGTOWN FOR 78 YEARS AND IT'S LIKE SHE WAS NEVER HERE. WHEN SHE DIES IT WON'T MATTER TO OUR TOWN BECAUSE SHE'S LIKE A SHADOW - SHE'S HERE BUT HAS NO SUBSTANCE. IT'S LIKE HER MAIN PURPOSE IS TO GET OLD AND DIE SO SHE CAN FILL UP A HOLE IN THE GROUND FOR ETERNITY. I GUESS I'M SAYING SHE NEVER GETS INVOLVED IN ANYTHING. SHE NEVER MAKES A DIFFERENCE IN ANYBODY'S LIFE - WELL, I SHOULD SAY THAT ANOTHER WAY - SHE NEVER SEEMS TO <u>TRY</u> TO MAKE A DIFFERENCE IN ANYBODY'S LIFE. SHE DOES MAKE A DIFFERENCE IN MY FAMILY'S LIFE BECAUSE WE ALL FEEL SORRY FOR HER AND THAT MAKES US SAD. I DON'T THINK SHE MEANS TO MAKE US SAD BUT THEN I

CAN'T REMEMBER A TIME SHE EVER TRIED TO MAKE US FEEL ANYWAY AT ALL. SHE DOESN'T VOTE SO SHE SURE DOESN'T HELP THINGS THAT WAY.

I MOW HER YARD EVEY WEEK ALL SUMMER LONG. I DO IT BECAUSE I WANT TO - SHE'S OLD - I DON'T EXPECT TO BE PAID - I WOULDN'T TAKE PAY BECASE IT'S SOMETHING I JUST WANT TO DO. BUT SHE SELDOM EVER SAYS THANKS - SOMETIMES SHE HAS A PLATE OF SUGAR COOKIES AND SAYS I CAN HAVE ONE IF I WANT BUT ITS NOT REALLY GIVEN TO ME WITH ANY SENSE OF APPRECIATION YOU KNONW. SHE JUST SITS BACK AND WATCHES - OBSERVES - THE WORLD GOING BY. IT'S LIKE SHE'S HELPLESS BUT ITS SOMETHING MORE THAN THAT. DOC SAYS SHE REALLY ISN'T DEPRESSED.

WHAT WILL HER OBITUARY SAY? "SHE WAS BORN, SHE LIVED, SHE DIED, THE WORMS ARE NOW ENJOYING HER FLESH (SHE FINALLY MADE A DIFFERENCE!!)."

AGE 8 [GRADE 6]

I'VE BEEN THINKING A LOT RECENTLY ABOUT BUTCHIE AND MISS BARRY. EVERYBODY HATES BOTH OF THEM - WELL, MOM AND POP AND I DON'T HATE PEOPLE AND I DOUBT IF PARSON HATES THEM EITHER CONSIDERING HIS CONNECTIONS, BUT THOSE WHO ARE PRONE TO HATE, REALLY DO TRULY HATE THEM BOTH.

BUTCHIE STEALS AND BEATS UP ON KIDS ALL THE TIME. IF HE CAN'T STEAL IT, HE SEEMS TO ENJOY RUINING OR BREAKING IT. FOR SOME REASON I'VE NEVER BEEN THE RECIPIENT OF ONE OF HIS FAMOUS THRASHINGS. I SUPPOSE THAT'S BEEN GOOD FOR MY HEALTH BUT BAD FOR MY IMAGE. HE CUSSES ALL THE TIME AND CALLS EVERYBODY BAD NAMES. IF HE LIVED WITH MOM SHE'D USE UP A WHOLE BAR OF LYE SOAP EVERY WEEK JUST WASHING OUT HIS MOUTH. (ON SUCH OCCASSIONS WHEN I HAVE PERSONALLY LET A BAD WORD SLIP, I'VE TRIED TO EXPLAIN TO MOM THAT IT'S NOT REALLY MY MOUTH THAT'S AT FAULT BUT MY BRAIN. SHE SAYS MY MOUTH IS AS CLOSE TO MY BRAIN AS SHE CAN GET SO THAT WILL

HAVE TO DO. BUT I GUESS THAT'S A SIDE TRIP.) [DIGRESSING STARTED EARLY, YOU SEE.]
    I DON'T THINK - NOW THERE'S A STRANGE PHRASE - OF COURSE I THINK . . . LET ME START OVER - I BELIEVE HE HAS PROBABLY NEVER WORKED TO EARN SO MUCH AS A NICKEL IN HIS LIFE - HE JUST TAKES WHAT HE WANTS. HE'S PROBABLY THE ONLY ONE WHO SPENDS MORE TIME IN THE PRINCIPAL'S OFFICE THAN ME. THAT DOESN'T SOUND SO GOOD, DOES IT. ANYWAY, I'M NEVER THEIR BECAUSE I'VE HURT ANYBODY OR BEEN MEAN OR NOT CARRIED OUT MY RESPONSIBILITIES. IT'S USUALLY JUST DIFFERENCES OF OPINION BETWEEN THE TEACHERS AND ME.
    THEN THERE'S MISS BARRY THE 4TH GRADE TEACHER. SHE AND BUTCHIE ARE A LOT ALIKE - OH, MISS BARRY DOESN'T STEAL (AS FAR AS I KNOW, ANYWAY) BUT SHE REALLY HURTS KIDS. SHE TREATS STUDENTS RUDELY. SHE IS SARCASTIC. SHE NEVER PRAISES ANYONE. NO ONE'S WORK IS EVER GOOD ENOUGH. SHE YELLS ALL DAY LONG. POP SAYS SOME PEOPLE THINK THEY HAVE TO MAKE KIDS AFRAID OF THEM IN ORDER TO KEEP CONTROL OF THEM. WELL, KIDS ARE AFRAID OF HER AND SHE DOES CONTROL THEM, NO DOUBT ABOUT THAT, BUT THEN MISS DISTLEMEYER CONTROLS KID, TOO, AND I'VE NEVER HEARD HER RAISE HER VOICE AND SHE'D NEVER SAY HATEFUL THINGS TO HER STUDENTS.
    REMEMEBER, DI, HOW LAST YEAR MISS BARRY HIT MY KNUCKLES WITH HER YARD STICK BECAUSE MY WRITING WAS SOLPPY. I GOT INTO A LITTLE TROUBLE WHEN I GRABBED IT FROM HER AND BROKE IT INTO THREE PIECES. BOY, I'VE NEVER BEEN SO POPULAR IN ALL MY LIFE! THE TROUBLE WAS WORTH IT. WHEN I TOLD POP ABOUT IT [AND I ALWAYS TRIED TO TELL HIM ABOUT MY 'INCIDENTS' BEFORE HE HEARD ABOUT THEM ELSEWHERE] HE RUBBED HIS MOUTH AND COUGHED - WELL, REALLY IT WAS A CHUCKLLE AND A SMILE HE WAS TRYING TO COVER UP - I COULD TELL - ANYWAY, HE REMINDED ME ABOUT

TREATING EVERYBODY WITH RESPECT AND THEN NEVER
BROUGHT IT UP AGAIN. I OVERHEARD MOM AND POP
GIGGLING ABOUT IT AFTER I WENT TO BED AND HE DID
GO SEE MR. MARTIN ABOUT IT. HER YARDSTICK WAS NOT
REPLACED.
    SO MUCH FOR THE CERTAINTIES OF LIFE I'VE BEEN
SEARCHING FOR. JOHN CALLS HER "MRS. HITLER." HE'S
ANOTHER GUY I DON'T UNDERSTAND (HITLER, NOT
JOHN). HE JUST WENT OUT AND TOOK WHOLE
COUNTRIES WHEN HE WANTED THEM, KILLING MILLIONS
OF PEOPLE - MANY OF THEM HIS OWN - ALONG THE WAY.
IT'S INTERESTING TO THINK THAT HITLER, MISS BARRY
AND BUTCHIE ALL BELONG TO THE SAME GROUP. AS BAD
AS HITLER WAS, HE REALLY NEVER EFFECTED MY DAY TO
DAY LIFE THE WAY MISS BARRY DID. GINNY [MY BEST
FRIEND SINCE AGE TWO, WHO WAS A GIRL AND WHO – ALL
QUITE UNBELIEVABLY TO ME AT EIGHT OR TWELVE OR
EVEN EIGHTEEN – WOULD SOMEDAY BE MY WIFE] SAYS THE
THREE OF THEM ARE EVIL. I'M NOT SURE ANYBODY REALLY
CLEARLY KNOWS WHAT EVIL MEANS. IT MAKES MORE
SENSE TO ME TO CALL THEM <u>DESTROYERS.</u>

AGE 9 [GRADE 8]

    I KNOW I'VE SAID IT BEFORE, DI, BUT I MUST BE
JUST ABOUT THE LUCKIEST BOY IN THE WORLD WHEN IT
COMES TO THE GROWN-UPS IN MY LIFE (WELL, EXCEPT
FOR MISS BARRY AND OLD LADY BLASTON OUT AT THE
COUNTY HOME). I USED TO BELIEVE THAT MY REAL
MOTHER AND FATHER WENT AND DIED ON ME ON
PURPOSE BUT NOW THAT I'M OLDER AND MORE MATURE,
I UNDERSTAND THAT WASN'T THEIR CHOICE - THEY
DIDN'T LEAVE ME ALONE INTENTIONALLY. WHAT THEY
DID LEAVE ME, HOWVER, WAS THIS NEEDLESSLY POWERFUL
BRAIN. NOBODY NEEDS THIS MUCH INTELLIGENCE. I
SURE WISH I HAD A LOT LESS, BUT THAT'S ANOTHER
STORY. WHAT I WAS GETTING TO SAY WAS THAT THEY

GAVE ME PLEANTY OF SMARTS AND A BODY THAT'S REALLY OKAY (THOUGH A LITTLE TALLER WOULD BE NICE IN CASE YOUR LISTENING, GOD).

AND THEN THERE'S MOM AND POP FRANKLIN - THEY JUST TOOK ME IN AS A TODDLER JUST BECAUSE THEY WANTED ME. NOBODY PAID THEM. NOBODY MADE THEM DO IT. THEY JUST TOOK ME IN AND THEY WERE OLD. [THE COUPLE HAD BEEN MY BABYSITTERS DURING THE SIX MONTHS I HAD LIVED IN SPRINGTOWN WITH MY PARENTS WHO WERE BOTH PH.DS. MOTHER TAUGHT AT THE LITTLE COLLEGE, THERE. THEY DIED IN A HOUSE FIRE. MOM AND POP FRANKLIN WERE 50 AND 60 RESPECTIVELY WHEN THEY TOOK ME IN AS A HYPERACTIVE TWO YEAR OLD – GOING ON THIRTY.] THAT WAS JUST LIKE THEM THOUGH. THEY ARE SO KIND. THEY LOVE EVERYBODY AND EVERYBODY LOVES THEM (US!).

IN TERMS OF MONEY-WEALTH, THEY ARE THE POOREST PARENTS IN TOWN BUT THEY STILL PUT BACK MONEY EVERY WEEK TO HELP THOSE WHO ARE LESS FORTUNATE THAN WE ARE. EVERY WEEK - USUALLY ON SUNDAY AFTERNOONS - WE DO SOMETHING HELPFUL FOR SOMEBODY - MOW THEIR YARD IF THEY CAN'T, SPADE THEIR GARDEN, WEED THEIR FLOWERS, SHOVEL THEIR SNOW, WASH AND IRON, TAKE THEM A HOT MEAL, CLEAN THEIR HOUSE, FIX FENCES, SOMETIMES JUST SIT AND TALK WHEN THEY ARE LONELY OR SAD. THE LIST JUST GOES ON AND ON. I LOVE DOING THAT STUFF. IT GIVES ME THE MOST WONDERFUL FEELING I CAN IMAGINE. (JOHN SAYS SEX WILL BE A BETTER FEELING, BUT I'M NOT SURE HOW HE KNOWS THAT. HE STILL BELIEVES WOMEN GET PREGNANT FROM KISSING IN THE DARK) I GUESS WHEN DOC EXPLAINED SEX TO ME HE LEFT OUT THE PART ABOUT GREAT FEELINGS. I'LL HAVE TO ASK POP. HE'LL BE HAPPY TO EXPLAIN THAT PART TO ME. [SURE, HE WILL, CRAIGY!]

I THINK ONE OF THE BEST THINGS ABOUT BEING A MEMBER OF THIS FAMILY IS PRESENTS - OH, WE DON'T GET VERY MANY, BUT WE ALWAYS MAKE THEM FOR EACH OTHER. WE NEVER BUY THEM. IT DOESN'T REALLY EVER

MATTER WHAT IT IS - IT'S JUST SO PRECIOUS BECAUSE SOMEONE PUT SO MUCH TIME AND LOVE INTO IT. JOHN GOT A NEW 22 RIFLE FOR HIS BIRTHDAY. HE TALKS ABOUT IT ALL THE TIME BUT HE'S NEVER ONCE MENTIONED THAT IT WAS A GIFT OF LOVE - MAYBE IT WASN'T. I SURE HOPE IT WAS.

IT HAS BEEN MY OBSERVATION (WELL, MY OBVERSATION*S*, REALLY) THAT IF YOU HAVEN'T SPENT A LOT OF TIME CREATING SPECIAL GIFTS FOR SOMEBODY ELSE, YOU NEVER REALLY SEEM TO UNDERSTAND HOW PRECIOUS A GIFT IS. AND THAT SECOND OBSERVATION IS THIS: I REALLY FEEL SORRY FOR THE POOR RICH KIDS (WHAT AN INTERESTING IDEA - POOR RICH KIDS). ANYWAY, I REALLY FEEL SORRY FOR THEM BECAUSE WHEN THEY WANT SOMETHING NEW THEY HAVE TO GO OUT AND BUY IT. WHEN I WANT SOMETHING NEW, I GET TO MAKE IT - I PLAN IT ALL OUT, FIGURE WHERE TO GET THE PARTS OR MATERIAL, FIND WAYS OF EARNING MONEY IF I NEED ANY, AND THEN I PUT IT ALL TOGETHER - I CREATE IT. HECK (WOOPS! SORRRY, GOD) I HAVE TWO BICYCLES I DIDN'T EVEN REALLY WANT - I JUST HAVE SO MUCH FUN MAKING THEM. POP AND I ARE GOING TO TAKE THEM OUT TO THE COUNTY HOME FOR THE KIDS IF I CAN CONVINCE OLD LADY BLASTON TO LET THEM HAVE THEM. MAYBE DOC WILL TELL HER THEY NEED THEM FOR PELVIC EXCERCISE - THEN SHE COULD HARDLY REFUSE.

I GUESS I GOT OFF TRACK SOMEWHERE. I JUST THOUGHT OF THIS: "GETTING OFF TRACK IS LIKE DISCOVERING A WONDER-FILLED NEW PATH IN THE WOODS." I'LL TELL PARSON THAT AND HE CAN USE IT FOR A SERMON TOPIC (OR AT LEAST A METAPHORE - I'VE DISCOVERED THAT ALL MINISTERS REALLY LOVE METAPHORES).

ANYWAY, I WAS TALKING ABOUT GOOD PEOPLE IN MY LIFE AND MY POINT WAS GOING TO BE THIS: I DON'T BELIEVE GOING TO CHURCH DEFINES YOU AS BEING A GOOD PERSON - PARSON MIGHT NOT EVEN ARGUE THAT

ONE FOR LONG. I BELIEVE A GOOD PERSON IS SOMEBODY WHO TRULY GETS A HEART-WARMING KICK OUT OF BEING HEPFUL TO OTHER PEOPLE. THAT'S INTERESTING BECAUSE IT'S ALMOST LIKE MY DEFINITION OF SUCCESS: "HAVING LIVED EVERYDAY TO IMPROVE THE LOT OF MANKIND OR AT LEAST THOSE FOLKS CLOSE ENOUGH FOR YOU TO REACH." GOOD AND SUCCESSFUL PEOPLE ARE THE ONES WHO BUILD A BETTER WORLD - THAT'S WHY I CALL THEM <u>BUILDERS</u>.

    LOTS OF FOLKS SEEM TO HAVE THAT ALL MESSED UP IN THEIR HEADS. GROWN-UPS ARE ALWAYS ASKING ME WHAT I'M GOING TO <u>BE</u> WHEN I GROW UP - AS IF WHAT <u>JOB</u> YOU DO IS THE MOST IMPORTANT BIG DEAL IN LIFE - LIKE YOUR SUCCESS IN LIFE DEPENDS ON YOUR JOB. I'VE DECIDED THAT I'M NEVER GOING TO ASK KIDS THAT QUESTION. INSTEAD, I'LL ASK: "WHAT'S YOUR PLAN FOR MAKING PEOPLE'S LIVES BETTER?" OR MAYBE "WHAT'S YOUR PLAN FOR HELPING MAKE THE WORLD A BETTER PLACE?" I'M SURE WHAT YOU ASK A KID ABOUT SUCH STUFF TURNS HIM IN THAT DIRECTION.

    HERE I AM NINE YEARS OLD AND ALRADY I'M A FULL-BLOWN SUCCESS BACAUSE EVERYDAY I REALLY DO ENJOY HELPING OTHERS. WOW!!!! SOMETIOMES I BOGGLE MY OWN MIND, AND, DI, YOU'D BETTER BELIEVE THAT IT TAKES SOME TREMENDOUS BOGGLING TO ACCOMPLISH THAT.

AGE 9 ½ [GRADE 9]
    OKAY, DI, HERE'S MY MOST RECENT REVELATION - YOU HAVE PROBABLY ALREADY PICKED UP ON IT BECAUSE I'M SURE IT'S ALL IN HERE IN BITS AND PIECES. (I WONDER HOW A 'BIT' IS DIFFERENT FROM A 'PIECE' AND WHY THAT PHRASE - BITS AND PIECES - REQUIRES BOTH WORDS TO MAKE IT ACCURATE?)

    AFTER YEARS OF CONSIDERATION AND OBSERVATION, I'VE FOUND THERE ARE FOUR BASIC TYPES OF PEOPLE - WELL, AT LEAST IN SO FAR AS HOW THEY

CONTRIBUTE TO THE HAPPINESS OR SADNESS - THE LIFE OR DEATH, REALLY - OF HUMANITY.

FIRST ARE THE MARY ANNS OF THE WORLD - <u>THE PEOPLE USERS</u>, I'VE DECIDED TO CALL THEM. THEY USE YOU UNTIL YOU HAVE NOTHING LEFT THEY WANT AND THEN THEY THROW YOU OUT LIKE SO MUCH RANCID MEAT. THEY ARE FULLY SELF-CENTERED PEOPLE AND NEVER EVEN SEEM TO CONSIDER THE FACT THAT OTHER PEOPLE'S NEEDS ARE LEGITIMATE, IMPORTANT AND DESERVE TO BE MET. THE PEOPLE USER ONLY DOES FOR HIMSELF. TAKEN TO ITS LOGICAL EXTREME, IF WE WERE ALL PEOPLE USERS, NO ONE WOULD EVER HELP MEET ANYBODY ELSE'S NEEDS AND THE HUMAN SPECIES WOULD JUST DIE OUT.

SO, THE FIRST GROUP IS <u>PEOPLE USERS</u>. THEN THERE ARE THE MRS. STEPHENS - THEY JUST SIT ON THE SIDELINES OF LIFE WATCHING IT GO BY. (THAT'S PRETTY GOOD! - WHAT I SAID, I MEAN, NOT THE ACTIVITY.) THEY NEVER MAKE A DIFFERENCE. THEY NEVER HELP IMPROVE THE HUMAN CONDITION AND OFTEN MAKE IT WORSE BY NOT ATTENDING TO THE ILLS OF THEIR NEIGHBORS. I'M NOT SURE IF THEY DON'T WANT TO BE HELPFUL OR IF SOMETHING JUST HOLDS THEM BACK. ONE DAY I'LL STUDY ABOUT THAT. MAYBE I CAN FIND A WAY TO GET THEM OFF THEIR BUTTS (OPPS! SORRY GOD.). MAYBE IF THEY WERE HAPPIER PEOPLE THEY WOULD WANT TO BE MORE HELPFUL, BUT THEN, I BELIEVE IT'S THROUGH BEING HELPFUL THAT WE REALLY BECOME HAPPY IN THE FIRST PLACE - IT'S A DILEMMA ABOUT WHICH HAS TO COME FIRST. IT'S LIKE THE CHICKEN OR THE EGG THINGY. (I'VE SOLVED THAT, BY THE WAY. THE THING THAT CAME FIRST WAS THE EGGPLANT! - HA! HA!)

I CALL THE MRS. STEPHENSES OF THE WORLD, THE <u>OBSERVERS</u> - IT'S DIFFERENT FROM BEING DEPRESSED LIKE MRS. LEMPKE - BEING AN OBSERVER IS MORE LIKE THE ULTIMATE ATTEMPT TO REMAIN SEPARATE, UNCONNECTED FROM OTHER HUMAN BEINGS. I IMAGINE

IT'S BASED ON FEAR. THEY ARE PROBABLY EXTREMELY SCARED OF SOME ASPECT OF SOCIAL INTERACTION WHEREAS THE DEPRESSED PERSON SEEMS TO BE TRYING TO KEEP HIS ANGER UNDER CONTROL (OR SO SAYS FREUD. I'LL BET ON SOME KIND OF BRAIN FUNCTION PROBLEM, MYSELF.)

 THE THIRD GROUP INCLUDES THE BARRY/BUTCHIE/HITLER TYPES OF THE WORLD - THE <u>DESTROYERS</u>. THEY'RE THE ULTIMATE SELFISH, NON-COMPASSIONATE BEINGS IN OUR WORLD. THEY HURT OTHERS WITH NO REMORSE. THEY TAKE WHAT THEY WANT BECAUSE THEY SEEM TO BELIEVE ANYTHING THEY WANT IS RIGHTFULLY THEIRS.

 I IMAGINE THEIR MINDS ARE SHORT-CIRCUITED IN A SIMILAR WAY AS THOSE OF PEOPLE USERS BUT THEY TAKE IT TO AN EXTREME - THEY ARE MORE DIRECT, MORE OBVIOUS. IF THE WORLD WAS MADE UP OF DESTROYERS ONLY, EVENTUALLY THERE WOULD ONLY BE ONE PERSON LEFT - BECAUSE DESTROYERS EVEN LIKE TO DESTROY EACH OTHER - AND UNLESS I MISUNDERSTAND THE SEX TALK FROM DOC, THAT MEANS THERE WOULD EVENTUALLY BE NO ONE LEFT AT ALL.

 ONE MORE THING I JUST REMEMBERED ABOUT - MR. EASLY - HE'S RICH AND HE BOUGHT THE GAS STATION OUT AT THE CROSSROADS. THEN HE PUT THE GAS PRICE SO LOW - BELOW HIS OWN COST, ACTUALLY - THAT THE JOHNSONS COULDN'T COMPETE HERE IN TOWN AND THEY WENT OUT OF BUSINESS. THEN, EASLY PUT THE PRICE UP HIGHER THAN IT WAS TO START WITH. I PERSONALLY BAWLED HIM OUT ABOUT IT. HE SAID IT WAS JUST GOOD BUSINESS - FREE MARKET COMPETITION - AS IF BUSINESS AND LIVING A GOOD LIFE WERE SOMEHOW SEPARATE, AND PLAYED BY DIFFERENT RULES. I TOLD HIM I THOUGHT IT STUNK. WHAT ABOUT COOPERATION? SHOULDN'T COOPERATION AND HELPFULNESS BE MORE IMPORTANT THAN COMPETITION AND HURTFULNESS? HE SNORTED. I WAS REALLY STEAMED, SO I SNORTED RIGHT

BACK. [I LEARNED THAT A BASS SNORT HAS MUCH MORE IMPACT THAN A SOPRANO SNORT!!!]

IT'S ONLY THE BUILDERS THAT MAKE CONTINUED HUMAN EXISTENCE POSSIBLE. I MEAN A REALLY GREAT EXISTENCE - A GOOD LIFE - WHERE EVERYBODY HAS THEIR NEEDS MET, IT IS SAFE AND COMFORTABLE AND LOVING AND EVERYBODY GETS TO DEVELOP THEMSELVES SO THEY CAN MEET THEIR OWN PERSONAL POTENTIAL - LIKE IN MY HOME.

A WORLD FULL OF MARY ANN'S COULDN'T BE THAT WAY.

A WORLD FULL OF MISS BARRY'S AND MR. EASLEY'S COULDN'T BE THAT WAY.

A WORLD FULL OF MRS. STEPHENS COULD NOT BE THAT WAY.

BUT, DI, CAN YOU JUST IMAGINE WHAT A WONDERFUL WORLD IT WILL BE WHEN IT IS CHUCK FULL OF MOM AND POP FRANKLINS, AND DOCS AND PARSONS AND GINNYS. WOW!

SO, YOU SEE, DI, I HAVE MY WORK CUT OUT FOR ME. NEXT, I HAVE TO DISCOVER ALL THE POSITIVE TRAITS THAT BUILDERS HAVE THAT ARE PERTINENTLY DIFFERENT FROM THE NEGATIVE TRAITS ALL THE NON-BUILDERS HAVE. I SHOULD HAVE THAT WELL IN HAND BY MY TENTH BIRTHDAY. I ALREADY HAVE SOME IDEAS. IT'S SORT OF LIKE FOOTBALL. (PARSON AND HIS METAPHORS HAVE RUBBED OFF ON ME, I'M AFRAID!) LINEMEN SEEM TO ALL HAVE A BIT OF THE DESTROYER IN THEM. THEY REALLY LIKE KNOCKING AROUND THEIR COUNTERPARTS ON THE OTHER TEAM. I'VE FOUND THAT MANY OF THEM AREN'T REALLY VERY COMPASSIONATE GUYS EVEN OFF THE FIELD. THE BACKS ARE - IN MY EXPERIENCE - LIKE PEOPLE USERS - THEY TAKE ALL THE GLORY BUT REALLY THEY COULDN'T DO A THING WITHOUT THE LINE. THE FANS ARE THE OBSERVERS - THEY WATCH BUT THEY CAN NEVER MAKE MUCH DIFFERENCE - IN A PHYSICAL SENSE. THE COACH SHOULD BE THE BUILDER. COACH LASKY IS THAT - HE'S A

KIND, TEACHER. I'VE SEEN SOME COACHES WHO WERE AT LEAST PEOPLE USERS IF NOT DESTROYERS. WINNING IS ALL THAT EVER COUNTS TO THEM. THAT'S THE ATTITUDE THAT WILL DESTROY MANKIND, I'M SURE OF THAT. THEY SCARE ME.

OUT OF TIME. IT'S WEDNESDAY . . . AND TIME TO GO HELP MR. DEETS CARRY HIS GROCERIES HOME NOW. . . . I NEED TO CHECK ON HIS CANARY. SOMETIMES HE FORGETS TO PUT OUT FOOD AND WATER. HE'S PRETTY OLD. SEE YOU LATER.

AGE 9 [8TH GRADE]
OUR VOTERS JUST VOTED DOWN A REFERENDUM TO START A FAMILY GUIDANCE CLINIC IN OUR COUNTY. [MENTAL HEALTH CENTER] I THINK THE GUYS IN THE COURTHOUSE RAN THE CAMPAIGN ALL WRONG. I TRIED TO TELL THEM SO BEFORE THE VOTE. THEY SPOKE ABOUT ALL THE HUMAN SUFFERING THAT MENTAL ILLNESS AND FAMILY-LIVING PROBLEMS CAUSE FOLKS IN OUR COUNTY. IT'S NOT THAT I'M NOT COMPASSIONATE ABOUT THOSE THINGS - I REALLY AM - I HATE TO SEE ANYBODY SUFFER FOR ANY REASON - BUT LET'S FACE IT - THAT ARGUMENT ONLY REALLY HOLDS UP WITH US BUILDERS. UNFORTUNATELY, THERE ARE CLEARLY NOT ENOUGH BUILDERS AROUND HERE TO PASS SUCH A REFERENDUM.

I WROTE THE ADMINISTRATOR OF THE COUNTY HEALTH DEPARTMENT AND TOLD HIM HOW HE SHOULD DO IT THE NEXT TIME. HERE'S THE PITCH: "HAPPY, WELL-ADJUSTED PEOPLE ARE EASIER TO LIVE WITH AND COST THE TAXPAYERS LESS IN THE LONG RUN. THEY SUPPORT THEMSELVES, OBEY THE LAWS AND PAY TAXES RATHER THAN BEING IN JAIL AND ON RELIEF. IT DOESN'T REALLY MATTER IF YOU WANT TO HELP THE EMOTIONALLY DISTURBED PEOPLE BECAUSE YOU HAVE COMPASSION FOR THEM OR JUST BECAUSE YOU SELFISHLY WANT THEM TO ALL BECOME FOLKS WHO ARE EASY TO LIVE WITH AND WHO PULL THEIR OWN WEIGHT. EITHER WAY, PROVIDING

THIS CLINIC IS IN EVERYBODY'S BEST INTEREST." SEE, DI, EVEN THE MOST SELFISH FOLKS - THE DESTROYERS, OBSERVERS AND PEOPLE USERS WANT THEIR OWN LIVES TO BE HAPPIER, SAFER AND LESS FRUSTRATING, SO EVEN THEY WILL BUY THE IDEA THAT THAT CAN HAPPEN A WHOLE LOT EASIER IF THEY ARE LIVING AMONG HAPPY, HELPFUL, LAW ABIDING, EMPLOYED PEOPLE. SPENDING JUST A FEW BUCKS A YEAR TO MAKE THAT HAPPEN MAKES SENSE TO THE LOT OF THEM. MARK MY WORD, IF THEY USE THAT APPROACH NEXT TIME, WE'LL HAVE A FAMILY GUIDANCE CLINIC. [THEY DIDN'T AND WE DIDN'T!]

* * * * * * *

And so it was that before I turned ten, I felt sufficiently prepared to meet and improve the World. I had people's approaches to living pretty well figured out and narrowed down to a manageable four. I understood which 'styles' helped and which hindered the ongoing and developing human condition. I had designed for myself a daily living plan – my philosophy translated into behaviors. Actually, what I decided I had was a daily living plan that still needed some tweaking. It needed a concisely stated, all-encompassing philosophy that could guide me in my moment to moment decisions. Here are several passages that indicate the growth and development of that philosophic guidepost.

AGE 9 ½ [GRADE 9]
DI,
I'VE DECIDED THAT NOW THAT I'M PRACTICALLY GROWN UP THAT I NEED TO PUT DOWN IN BLACK AND WHITE WHAT MY PHILOSOPHY OF LIVING IS SO HERE GOES. I CALL <u>IT MY BUILDER'S WAY OF LIVING</u>. IT'S KIND OF LIKE MY STARTING POINT OR BASELINE.
EVERYDAY I:
1 - DO THE JOBS I HAVE TO DO (LIKE BRUSH MY TEETH, TAKE OUT THE TRASH, SET THE TABLE, GO TO SCHOOL AND DO THE WORK ASSIGNED, GO TO MY JOB AFTER SCHOOL AND ON SATURDAY, THINGS LIKE THAT)

2 - DO SOMETHING ESPECIALLY NICE FOR SOMEONE ELSE (SOMETHING NOT EXPECTED OR REQUIRED. DO IT ANONYMOUSLY WHENEVER POSSIBLE. TAKING CREDIT FOR A CHARITABLE ACT PUTS YOU IN THE LIMELIGHT - LIKE FEEDING YOUR EGO. THE EMPHASIS SHOULD JUST BE TO QUIETLY BE HELPFUL - NOT MAKE YOURSELF LOOK GOOD. THEN IT WOULDN'T BE A CHARITABLE ACT BUT A SELF-PROMOTIONAL ACT.)

3 - LEARN SOMETHING NEW EVERY DAY. (IT MAY JUST BE SOMETHING INTERESTING BUT WHO KNOWS WHEN IT MAY BE HELPFUL TO ME OR TO SOMEONE ELSE. "THERE ARE SO MANY THINGS TO LEARN ABOUT A SO LITTLE TIME IN WHICH TO LEARN THEM" - THAT'S A QUOTE FROM MOM.)

4 - DO SOMETHING - SOMETHING NICE - FOR MYSELF. (IT'S LIKE LEGITIMATE SELFISHNESS. I THINK IF YOU DON'T TAKE GOOD CARE OF YOURSELF LIKE THAT, YOU CAN'T DO YOUR BEST FOR OTHERS. - I LEARNED THAT FROM DOC.)

I MAY NEED TO REVISE IT WHEN I GET TO BE A GROWNUP BUT MOM AND POP SAY PROBABLY NOT. YOU CAN'T KNOW WHAT THE WORLD'S GOING TO BE LIKE LATER ON WITH ATOM BOMBS AND THINGS. MAYBE IT WILL NEED SOME REARRANGING. I'LL KEEP A CLOSE WATCH ON IT JUST IN CASE.

[NOT LONG AFTER THIS I FELT THE NEED FOR SOMETHING ELSE AND FELT THE AVAILABLE GUIDANCE NEEDED SOME TWEAKING BEFORE IT WOULD BE TRULY USEFUL.]

AGE 9 ½ [GRADE 9]
DI - I JUST CAME FROM PARSON'S. WE HAD A LONG TALK ABOUT LIVING A GOOD LIFE. (I THINK IT WAS ACTUALLY POP'S IDEA THAT THE TALK TAKE PLACE.) I'M LESS AND LESS INCLINED TO TAKE WHAT PARSON HAS TO SAY AS GOD'S TRUTH WITHOUT FIRST EXAMINING IT PRETTY CAREFULLY. THAT DRIVES HIM INSANE! (PARSON

NOT GOD - WELL, MAYBE GOD TOO, I CAN'T BE SURE ABOUT THAT.) IF THERE IS AN ALL-WISE GOD (AND, GOD, IF YOU ARE REALLY THERE, I ASSUME YOU WILL FORGIVE ME FOR HAVING SOME DOUBTS RIGHT NOW) I HAVE TO CONCLUDE THAT SOME - NO, MANY - OF HIS INTENTIONS HAVE BEEN GROSSLY MISINTERPRETED OR AT LEAST MIS-STATED BY THOSE WHO ARE SUPPOSEDLY IN A POSITION TO RECEIVE THEM. (WHO THEY ARE, HOW WE KNOW WHO THEY ARE, AND HOW THEY COME TO BE THAT, ARE TOPICS FOR ANOTHER DAY.)

PARSON KEEPS COMING BACK TO THE <u>GOLDEN RULE</u>, WHICH HE STATES THIS WAY: DO UNTO OTHERS WHAT YOU WOULD HAVE OTHERS DO UNTO YOU. TAKEN LITERALLY, THAT'S REALLY A PRETTY DANGEROUS STATEMENT IF YOU ASK ME. (AND NO ONE HAS, OF COURSE!) IT ONLY SEEMS LIKE A GOOD GUIDELINE FOR PEOPLE WHO ARE REALLY GOOD AND WISE PEOPLE TO BEGIN WITH. WHAT WOULD IT MEAN TO THE DESTROYERS? IT'S LOGICALLY INCOMPATIBLE WITH THEIR POSITION. THEY WOULD HAVE OTHERS GET OUT OF THEIR WAY OR DIE, SO THEY (THE DESTROYERS) CAN HAVE EVERYTHING THEY WANT. WHAT DESTROYERS WOULD HAVE OTHERS DO UNTO THEM IS TO GIVE THEM EVERYTHING THEY WANT. CLEARLY, THEY WOULD NOT THEN GIVE IT ALL BACK AS PER THE RULE. SAME FOR THE PEOPLE USER AND THE OBSERVER. AND EVEN US GOOD GUYS WOULD MAKE A SHAMBLES OF THE WORLD IF WE FOLLOWED THAT RULE TO THE LETTER. I'D REALLY LIKE TO HAVE A BABY RUTH CANDY BAR EVERY SINGLE DAY (THREE TIMES EVERY SINGLE DAY, IN FACT) BUT IF I DID THAT UNTO ALL THE OTHER KIDS HOW WOULD THAT HELP ANYTHING (EXCEPT THE BABY RUTH COMPANY AND DENTISTS, I SUPPOSE.)? ALL US KIDS WOULD HAVE TUMMY ACHES, WE'D LOSE OUR APPETITES AND FAIL TO EAT WHAT'S REALLY GOOD FOR US AND ON AND ON AND ON.

IT'S JUST NOT A SIMPLE THING, AND IN MY ESTIMATION, GOD NEEDS TO CHANGE HIS RULE. I'VE

THOUGHT A LOT ABOUT IT BUT I'M NOT SURE YET WHAT THE RULE SHOULD BE.

AGE 9 8/12   [GRADE 9]
    DI - THAT BLASTED (SORRY, GOD) GOLDEN RULE WILL BE THE DEATH OF ME. BETTY ANN, JIMMY'S FOUR-YEAR-OLD SISTER WANTED A BITE OF MY COOKIE THIS AFTERNOON, SO, I THOUGHT, "DO UNTO OTHERS WHAT I WOULD HAVE THEM DO UNTO ME." I BROKE THE COOKIE IN TWO AND GAVE HALF OF IT TO HER. HER MOTHER CALLED UP MOM AND COMPLAINED THAT I HAD TO STOP GIVING BETTY ANN SWEETS BEFORE SUPPER. SHE SEEMED REALLY ANGRY ABOUT IT. MAYBE THE RULE SHOULD REALLY SAY: "DO UNTO OTHERS ONLY THOSE THINGS THAT EVERYBODY ELSE IN THE WORLD THINKS YOU SHOULD DO FOR THEM." (AND THEN, ONLY AFTER A COMMITTEE MEETING OF ALL PARTIES EVEN REMOTELY CONCERNED!!!) I DID KNOW IT MIGHT RUIN HER APPETITE, BUT THE RULE DOESN'T SAY ANYTHING ABOUT THAT - IT SAYS "WHAT I WOULD HAVE OTHERS DO FOR ME" AND I'D SURE HAVE OTHERS GIVE ME HALF A COOKIE ANYTIME THE OPPORTUNITY AROSE. THIS GOLDEN RULE THING IS REALLY CONFUSING.

AGE 9 11/12 [GRADE 9]
    OKAY, GOD, HERE'S THE DEAL. I'LL CONCEDE THAT IF YOU'RE REALLY OUT THERE YOU HAVE TO BE A PRETTY SMART AND WISE GUY (OR WOMAN - HUMM - MORE THAN LIKELY AN 'IT' SINCE IF YOU ARE ALL ALONE IN THE GOD BUSINESS YOU'D THEREFORE NOT HAVE THE POSSIBILITY OF A WIFE, AND IF YOU EXIST FOREVER, YOU'D HAVE NO NEED FOR LITTLE GOD-KIDS TO CARRY ON FOR YOU, SO I GUESS GENDER IS IRRELEVANT.) WHAT WAS I SAYING. OH, YES. IF YOU EXIST, YOU'RE SMART AND WISE AND IF YOU'RE SMART AND WISE YOU'D NOT GIVE OUT A RULE THAT'S AS COMPLETELY USELESS AS I FIND THE GOLDEN RULE TO BE. THEREFORE, I HAVE CONCLUDED THAT YOUR

INTENTION HAS BEEN MISINTERPRETED AND KNOWING WHAT I KNOW ABOUT PEOPLE INTERACTING WITH OTHER PEOPLE, I THINK I UNDERSTAND WHAT YOU INTENDED THAT RULE TO REALLY BE. HERE IS WHAT I'M SURE YOU MEANT: "ONLY DO TO AND FOR YOURSELF AND OTHERS THOSE THINGS YOU HAVE GOOD REASON TO BELIEVE WILL BE BEST FOR ALL CONCERNED IN THE LONG RUN."

    I'VE GIVEN IT A LOT OF THOUGHT. I'VE WRITTEN AND RE-WRITTEN IT A HUNDRED TIMES (WELL, I DIDN'T ACTUALLY KEEP COUNT.). I'VE CHANGED IT AND ADDED TO IT. I'VE TRIED IT OUT IN EVERY FORM I HAD, AND THIS FORM HAS TO BE THE REAL RULE. I KNOW IT'S A WHOLE LOT MORE COMPLICATED AND IT CALLS FOR EACH PERSON TO WORK REALLY HARD AT GATHERING ALL THE FACTS BEFORE HE ACTS, BUT I THINK THIS IS A MUCH MORE USEFUL - PRAGMATICALLY PRACTICAL - RULE. (YOU MAY CALL IT THE "PLATINUM RULE" IF YOU WANT TO AND I DON'T CARE IF YOU GIVE ME ANY CREDIT FOR IT - EVEN THOUGH I HAVE PUT IN A GREAT DEAL OF TIME.)

AGE 9 11/12 [GRADE 9]

    HEY GOD! CRAIGY, HERE. I RAN THE NEW PLATINUM RULE PAST DOC, PARSON, AND MOM AND POP. NONE OF THEM SEEMED TO BELIEVE I PUT IT ALL TOGETHER - WELL, THEY KNOW I DON'T LIE SO I DIDN'T MEAN IT THAT WAY (JUST IN CASE YOU WERE WONDERING). I MEANT THEY WERE AMAZED - IMPRESSED, I THINK. PARSON SAID HE'D USE IT IN A SERMON. I TOLD HIM IT WOULD TAKE AT LEAST FOUR TO PROPERLY PRESENT IT. HE PATTED ME ON THE HEAD - I HATE THAT!! (I SUPPOSE IT'S OKAY TO HATE A BEHAVIOR, ISN'T IT? I DON'T HATE PARSON BECAUSE HE DOES IT, YOU UNDERSTAND.) I GUESS I'LL JUST HAVE TO OUTLINE THE SERMONS FOR HIM SO HE GETS THE RIGHT IDEA ABOUT IT ALL.

    IT'S THE WORD "BEST" IN THAT RULE THAT REQUIRES THE MOST WORK - THE MOST RESPONSIBILITY,

I GUESS WOULD BE MORE ACCURATE. IT'S ALSO 'BEST' ACCORDING TO WHOM OR WHAT THAT IS THE PART THAT MAKES IT OPEN TO A LOT OF INTERPRETATIONS.

SO, I'VE STARTED MAKING A LIST OF VALUES AND BELIEFS AND BEHAVIORS THAT MAKE THINGS BETTER FOR MANKIND AND THE WORLD, AND THEN THE OTHER SIDE OF IT - THE VALUES AND BELIEFS AND BEHAVIORS THAT ARE HARMFUL AND DESTRUCTIVE. THAT WAY THE TERM 'BEST' WILL BE DEFINED PRETTY WELL, I THINK. IT'S HARD TO BELIEVE THAT ONE LITTLE RULE CAN REQUIRE SO MUCH WORK. I CAN'T TALK WITH MY FRIENDS ABOUT IT BECAUSE THEY EITHER AREN'T INTERESTED OR THEY DON'T UNDERSTAND.

IF IT'S THAT THEY DON'T UNDERSTAND, I'LL HAVE TO FIND WAYS OF SIMPLIFYING IT BECAUSE I THINK IT'S IMPORTANT FOR KIDS TO KNOW ALL THIS STUFF AS EARLY IN LIFE AS POSSIBLE. MAYBE IF I WERE JUST DUMBER, I'D UNDERSTAND HOW TO SAY IT BETTER SO THEY COULD UNDERSTAND IT - OF COURSE, IF WERE DUMBER, I'VE CONCLUDED, I MIGHT NOT HAVE THOUGHT IT UP IN THE FIRST PLACE. WHAT AN INTERESTING CONUNDRUM (I'M NOT SURE THAT'S THE RIGHT WORD BUT NO TIME TO LOOK IT UP NOW - I GOT A GAME OF MARBLES WITH CHUCK AND BILLY IN SIX MINUTES. I GOT TO PUT SOME ROSIN ON MY RIGHT THUMBNAIL. I HAVE FOUND THAT REALLY HELPS MAKE STRAIGHT SHOTS. CHUCK ALWAYS SPITS ON HIS THUMB TO HELP HIM SO I DON'T CONSIDER THE ROSIN CHEATING. SPIT, BY THE WAY, ACTUALLY JUST MAKES HIS NAIL SLIPPERY AND HIS SHOTS GO AWRY. HE DOESN'T SEEM TO PAY ATTENTION TO THE RESULTS OF HIS PROCEDURE. HE'S JUST SO CAUGHT UP IN THE PROCEDURE HE OVERLOOKS WHAT HAPPENS. I SUPPOSE THAT WILL ASSIST HIM IF HE EVER BECOMES A TEACHER.)

* * * * * * *

Knowing as I did even at age nine that each person had his or her own unique turn to defining just about every important word, it seemed particularly important to carefully define each word and phrase related to "the rule." Since people often seem to understand what they *see* better than what they *hear*, I set out to exemplify, in my behavior, the positive values. I had discovered. [Craigy's "Platinum Rule" is the basis of the parenting book titled, *The One Rule Plan For Family Happiness*. In it, the application of the concept is described within the family setting.]

    The agreements that follow in the next section amplify "The Rule" and represent a further attempt at clarifying and specifying aspects of social interaction that seem to be crucial.

SECTION THREE:
Twenty-four Positive Social Agreements

Topic One:
Basing one's life on love

AGE 5 [GRADE 1]
 I THINK THIS WAS PROBABLY THE MOST IMPORTANT DAY IN MY WHOLE LIFE, SO FAR, BUT I'M NOT COMPLETELY SURE WHY YET. I WAS AT THE FEED STORE BEFORE SCHOOL - WHERE THE MEN AND I DRINK COFFEE AND PLAY CHECKERS EVERY MORNING. (WELL, I DON'T DRINK COFFEE BUT I AM A MEAN CHECKER PLAYER). MR. GARTH WAS THERE - HE'S NEW AROUND HERE - BOUGHT THE SPRINGER PLACE ON THE OTHER SIDE OF TOWN. CAME FROM MISSISSIPPI I THINK. MAYBE ALABAMA. I'M NOT SURE.
 WELL, I WAS TRYING TO MAKE HIM FEEL WELCOME HERE SO I WENT UP TO HIM AND PUT OUT MY HAND FOR A SHAKE AND TOLD HIM WELCOME TO OUR LITTLE TOWN. THAT'S WHEN HE SAID IT AND THAT'S WHEN I WENT CRAZY. (BELIEVE ME, DI, GOING CRAZY IS <u>NEVER</u> THE THING TO DO.)
 HE SHOOK AND SMILED A REALLY NICE SMILE BUT

THEN HE SAID, "OH, YES, YOU'RE THE LITTLE WHITE BOY THAT LIVES WITH THAT OLD NIGGER MAN."

<u>OLD</u> I COULD HAVE ACCEPTED EVEN THOUGH IT SEEMED LIKE A NOT NEEDED PUT-DOWN THE WAY HE SAID IT. BUT HEARING HIM CALL MY WONDERFUL POP A NIGGER, SENT ME INTO A RAGE. I DON'T REMEMBER A LOT ABOUT WHAT HAPPENED NEXT ALTHOUGH SECOND HAND REPORTS ALL SEEM TO TELL IT THE SAME WAY. IT SEEMS I FLEW AT HIM, HITTING AND KICKING AND SCREAMING THAT I HATED HIM. IT'S MY BEST ESTIMATE THAT IT TOOK FOUR GROWN MEN TO DRAG ME OFF THE MAN.

I REMEMBER DOC FINALLY PICKED ME UP AND PUT ME UNDER HIS ARM AND CARRIED ME HOME. HE SAT ME DOWN ON THE BACK STEPS AND TOLD ME TO WAIT RIGHT THERE WHILE HE WENT INSIDE AND TALKED WITH MOM AND POP. I JUST SAT THERE AND CRIED LIKE A LITTLE KID. I HAD A STRANGE FEELING THAT I HAD JUST DONE SOMETHING TERRIBLE AND SOMETHING WONDERFUL ALL AT THE SAME TIME.

I WAS STILL ON THE STEPS WHEN DOC LEFT. HE DIDN'T SPEAK BUT HE DID LEAN DOWN ANDS KISS ME ON THE TOP OF MY HEAD - A MIXED MESSAGE TO BE SURE - DOC AND I <u>ALWAYS</u> TALK ABOUT EVERYTHING - LIKE YESTERDAY WHEN WE DISCUSSED THE PROS AND CONS OF CIRCUMCISION.

ANYWAY POP CAME OUT ALONE AND SAT BESIDE ME. WHEN IT IS JUST POP ALONE, IT MEANS IT IS GOING TO BE A REALLY SERIOUS TALK. HE HANDED ME HIS RED HANDKERCHIEF AND WAITED FOR ME TO DRY MY FACE BEFORE HE STARTED.

HE SAID WE HAD A SERIOUS PROBLEM. I SAID I FIGURED AS MUCH AND NODDED. HE SAID DOC HAD EXPLAINED WHAT HAD HAPPENED AND HE RETOLD THE STORY TO ME AND ASKED IF THAT'S HOW I REMEMBERED IT. I SAID YES IT WAS. POP NODDED. (A GOOD SIGN, I THOUGHT.)

THEN HE STARTED TALKING. HE DIDN'T SOUND

ANGRY - BUT THEN I CAN'T EVER REMEMBER POP SOUNDING ANGRY. ANYWAY HE SAID HE WOULD ALLOW ME TO BELIEVE MOST ANYTHING I WANTED TO BELIEVE AND HE KNEW ONCE I LEFT HIS HOME I <u>WOULD</u> BELIEVE ANYTHING I WANTED TO, BUT AS LONG AS I WAS A PART OF HIS FAMILY HE WOULD NOT ALLOW ME TO HATE OTHER PEOPLE. I SAID "BUT…" AND HE SHUSHED ME QUIET. HE SAID, "I KNOW THAT THE MAN CALLED ME A DESPICABLE NAME THE WAY YOU AND I THINK OF THAT WORD. BUT WE DON'T KNOW WHAT HE MEANT BY IT. AND EVEN IF HE MEANT THE VERY WORST BY IT, FRANKLINS DON'T HATE HIM FOR SAYING IT. FRANKLINS DON'T HATE ANYONE FOR ANY REASON. IS THAT CLEAR, SON?"

I LOOKED UP AT HIM AND BEGAN CRYING ALL OVER AGAIN. I NODDED AND SAID "YES, SIR. THAT'S CLEAR." HE REACHED OUT AND I SNUGGLED UP AS CLOSE AS I COULD GET TO HIM. I ALWAYS FEEL SO SAFE IN HIS BIG STRONG ARMS.

WE JUST STAYED CLOSE LIKE THAT FOR A LONG TIME. HE NEVER THANKED ME FOR STANDING UP FOR HIM BUT I GOT THE IDEA HE WAS VERY PLEASED TO KNOW HOW MUCH HE MEANT TO ME. TOMORROW I HAVE TO GO AND APOLOGIZE TO MR. GARTH. I AM TRYING TO FIGURE OUT IF I SHOULD TRY TO EXPLAIN TO HIM <u>WHY</u> I DID IT. I SUPPOSE HE KNOWS. I HOPE I DIDN'T HURT HIM TOO BAD. I DO REMEMBER GETTING IN A FEW GOOD BLOWS TO WHERE A GUY NEVER WANTS TO GET A FEW GOOD BLOWS.

I HAVE DECIDED THAT I REALLY DO NOT HATE HIM. I REALLY DID HATE WHAT HE SAID AND I GUESS I STILL DO, EVEN IF MAYBE HE DIDN'T MEAN ANYTHING AS BAD BY IT AS I IMAGINED HE DID. I KNOW WE FRANKLINS LOVE PEOPLE - THAT'S JUST ABOUT THE BEST THING ABOUT MY FAMILY - WE LOVE EVERYBODY AND JUST ABOUT EVERYBODY I KNOW SEEMS TO LOVE US BACK. I'M AFRAID I GAVE OUR FAMILY A BIG BLACK MARK AROUND HERE BY WHAT I DID. I CAN'T UNDO THAT. THAT'S WHY I

TOLD POP I THOUGHT I SHOULD APOLOGIZE TO MR. GARTH AT THE FEED STORE IN FRONT OF ALL THE MEN WHO HEARD ME SAY IT. THAT WILL BE THE HARDEST THING I'VE EVER HAD TO DO, BUT I BELIEVE IT IS THE PROPER THING TO DO. IT WILL BE HARD TO SLEEP TONIGHT.

AGE 9   [GRADE 8]

    EIGHTH GRADE IS NOT TURNING OUT TO BE ONE OF THE MOST POSITIVE EXPERIENCES OF MY LIFE, DI. IT'S VERY STRANGE - EVERYBODY IS SUDDENLY A SNOB. THE GIRLS ALL TALK BADLY ABOUT EACH OTHER BEHIND EACH OTHER'S BACKS. THE BOYS EXPEND THE MAJORITY OF THEIR CONVERSATIONAL ENERGIES TRYING TO ONE-UP EVERYBODY ELSE - ANOTHER WAY OF REALLY PUTTING EVERYBODY DOWN - BUT AT LEAST GUYS DO IT RIGHT TO EACH OTHER'S FACES. IT'S NOT A VERY HEALTHFUL ENVIRONMENT IN WHICH TO LIVE AND GROW. I HAVE TO ASSUME RELATIONSHIPS GET BETTER AFTER 8TH GRADE BECAUSE A WORLD BASED ON ALL THIS NEGATIVE STUFF COULDN'T POSSIBLY EXIST FOR LONG. I'VE CONCLUDED IT IS THE MOST INSECURE LOT OF HUMANITY I'VE YET ENCOUNTERED HERDED INTO ONE SMALL SPACE (PERHAPS THAT HELPS ACCOUNT FOR IT!). THE GIRLS SEEM MORE VICIOUS. IF THEY CAN MAKE ANOTHER GIRL CRY OR BREAK A BOY'S HEART THEY SEEM OVERJOYED. I SUPPOSE IT'S A SEARCH FOR SELF-WORTH THROUGH POWER AND POPULARITY. I SURE HOPE MY GENES ALLOW ME TO SKIP THAT STAGE. I WOULD FEEL POSITIVELY TERRIBLE (AN INTERESTING 2 WORD PHRASE!) EVERY NIGHT AS I LOOKED BACK OVER MY DAY IF I LIVED THAT WAY. THEY SEEM TO LIVE BY THE DESTROYER'S RULE: "DO BADLY UNTO OTHERS BEFORE THEY DO BADLY UNTO ME." A VISITOR FROM OUTER SPACE WOULD SURELY THINK 8TH GRADE WAS THE EARTHMAN'S TRAINING GROUND FOR FUTURE JOHN DILLENGERS AND AL CAPONES. IT'S VERY DIFFICULT TO BELIEVE MY MODELING OF POSITIVE

VALUES AMONG THEM MAKES ONE WHIT OF A DIFFERENCE BUT I WILL KEEP TRYING. I FIGURE WHEN THEY PUT ME DOWN AS BEING A 'GOODY-GOODY' FOR ACTING CIVIL (OR IS IT CIVILLY?) I ASSUME THEY ARE TRYING TO ALLEVIATE THEIR OWN GUILT THROUGH SOME FORM OF GROUP CONSENSUS. READING BACK OVER WHAT I'VE WRITTEN, IT IS HARDLY A NINE-YEAR-OLD'S PASSAGE, DI. UNFORTUNATELY, IT WAS CLEARLY NOT AN 8TH GRADER'S PASSAGE EITHER. I REALLY DON'T SEEM TO FIT IN ANYWHERE BUT AT HOME RIGHT NOW. THANK GOD FOR MOM AND POP AND ARNIE AND DOC - AND USUALLY, FOR PARSON ALTHOUGH RECENTLY HE IS BECOMING REALLY THICK HEADED ABOUT RELIGIOUS MATTERS.

[Arnie was an elderly, uneducated, "Mountain Man" Craigy befriended during the year he was nine. That story is chronicled in my book, *Zephyr in Pinstripes: The nine year-old boy with the size 18 brain*.]

POSITIVE, SOCIAL, AGREEMENT # 1:

I WILL build my life around love and I recognize that love is a one way characteristic with no expectation or requirement of being loved in return,

RATHER THAN allowing hate to guide me or cloud my direction and behavior,

BECAUSE hate can only destroy the human species while only love can preserve and enhance it.

Topic Two:
Love Must Be Guided By Appropriate Knowledge and Understanding

AGE 8 [Grade Six]

GINNY AND I WERE TALKING DOWN AT THE CREEK TODAY. WE DECIDED LIFE WILL BE A WHOLE LOT EASIER FOR US IF WE JUST LOVE EVERYBODY. THAT WAY THERE'S ONLY ONE GROUP OF PEOPLE WE HAVE TO DEAL WITH - THOSE WE LOVE. FOR HER 8TH BIRTHDAY MY PRESENT TO GINNY WAS EXPLAINING HOW YOU COULD LOVE SOMEBODY, SPECIFICALLY HER OLDER BROTHER, AND STILL NOT LIKE THE KIND OF PERSON THEY ARE.

SHE SAID IT WAS ONE OF THE BEST PRESENTS SHE HAD EVER RECEIVED. I'VE ALWAYS FELT THAT LEARNING SOMETHING NEW WAS LIKE A WONDER-FILLED PRESENT. GINNY AND I ARE A LOT ALIKE EVEN IF SHE IS A GIRL. ONE THING THAT AMAZES ME ABOUT HER IS THAT SHE REALLY DOESN'T EVEN MIND THAT SHE'S A GIRL. THAT'S PRETTY HARD TO FIGURE, BUT I SUPPOSE SHE'LL BE A LOT HAPPIER PERSON BECAUSE OF IT.

GINNY'S BROTHER, TOM, IS 24. HE'S NOT MARRIED AND CAN'T KEEP A JOB. HE DRINKS A LOT AND SMOKES - BOTH THINGS OUR <u>CHURCH OF THE BRETHREN</u> DOESN'T ALLOW. HE'S NOT ONE OF THE GOOD GUYS IN THIS WORLD. HIS MOTHER AND FATHER LOVE HIM A LOT AND THEY'VE ALWAYS LET HIM KNOW THAT, BUT THAT'S CLEARLY NOT BEEN ENOUGH. THEY ARE GOOD PEOPLE BUT THEY DON'T SEEM TO UNDERSTAND THAT THERE IS A LOT MORE TO BEING A GOOD PARENT THAN JUST LOVING YOUR KIDS. I'M SURE THEY HAVE NEVER TAKEN THE TIME TO STUDY CHILD GROWTH AND DEVELOPMENT OR EVEN READ ANY BOOKS ON IMPROVING FAMILY LIFE. DAVID (HE'S 22) TURNED OUT BETTER, I GUESS, HE MOVED TO CALIFORNIA WHEN HE WAS SEVENTEEN SO I BARELY REMEMBER HIM. GINNY, OF COURSE, IS GREAT, BUT I'VE OFTEN PERSONALLY GIVEN HER PARENTS SOME POINTERS ON RAISING HER. PEOPLE JUST DON'T DARE COUNT ON

HAVING SOMEBODY ELSE AROUND TO HELP YOU OUT LIKE THAT, THOUGH.

I GUESS WHAT I'M SAYING IS THAT IT SEEMS TO ME WE HAVE TO START OUT BY JUST PLAIN AND SIMPLY LOVING EVERYBODY BUT THAT'S NOT ENOUGH IF WE ALSO BELIEVE WE HAVE SOME RESPONSIBILITY FOR IMPROVING THIS HUMAN SPECIES WE BELONG TO. WE HAVE TO ENCOURAGE OURSELVES TO LEARN WHAT WE NEED TO KNOW SO WE CAN HELP IN THE RIGHT (PROVED) WAYS. I'LL BET YOU, DI, THAT NOT A SINGLE MAN DOWN AT THE FEED STORE EVEN KNOWS THERE ARE PROVEN GUIDELINES AVAILABLE THAT CAN HELP PARENTS RAISE GOOD, WELL-ADJUSTED CHILDREN. MAYBE THAT'S THE BIGGEST CRIME - NOT TAKING TIME TO FIND OUT IF THERE ARE ALREADY GOOD ANSWERS AVAILABLE TO HELP YOU DO THOSE THINGS YOU HAVE TO DO (LIKE BE A GOOD PARENT, OR A GOOD TEACHER, OR, EARLIER IN LIFE, A GOOD DATE OR FRIEND).

I GUESS THE MOST IMPORTANT SUBJECT IS NEVER EVEN TAUGHT IN SCHOOL - "WHAT KIND OF HELPFUL INFORMATION IS AVAILABLE AND WHERE TO FIND IT."

I'LL HAVE TO SPEAK WITH PRINCIPAL MARTIN ABOUT THAT. TIME FOR BED. I THINK I'LL SLEEP ON THE FLOOR IN THE KITCHEN IN FRONT OF THE OPEN DOOR - IT'LL BE COOLER THERE TONIGHT - THE BREEZE IS FROM THE SOUTH.

POSITIVE SOCIAL AGREEMENT # 2:

I WILL build my life on love and will guide it with the kinds of knowledge, experiences and expertise necessary to apply it appropriately,

RATHER THAN behaving on the devastating assumption that love needs no rational support for its helpful application,

BECAUSE, when you truly love, it becomes your responsibility to fully understand what is and is not helpful in those situations

that come up. (Example: There are parenting procedures that typically raise mentally healthy, happy, productive youngsters and there are those that do the opposite. Both can be administered through 'love' but the latter is also based on ignorance, which typically trumps love. Knowledge is the key to the effective administration of love, and its acquisition has to become more important than work, socializing with friends, or watching hour after hour of TV.)

Topic Three:
Making the survival and enhancement of the human species paramount in your life

AGE 7 [GRADE 5]
DEAR DI,
    TODAY MY TEACHER TOLD MARK THAT IF HE CONTINUED TO NOT DO HIS HOMEWORK GOD WOULD PUNISH HIM. I TOLD HER I THOUGHT THAT WAS A TERRIBLE THING TO TELL HIM AND THAT SHE SHOULD SPEAK TO HER MINISTER ABOUT HER BEHAVIOR AT HER EARLIEST CONVENIENCE. I SPENT MOST OF THE DAY WITH PRINCIPAL MARTIN. I WAS READING ABOUT THE MANY SPECIES OF ANIMALS THAT ARE NOW EXTINCT AND GOT TO WONDERING - WORRYING, I SUPPOSE - IF MANKIND WOULD BE EXTINCT TOO, SOMEDAY. IF THAT HAPPENS, I ASSUME IT WILL COME LONG AFTER I'M WORM FOOD, BUT THAT WAS NOT AT ALL REASSURING TO ME. IF THERE IS SOMETHING I CAN DO TODAY TO HELP MANKIND SURVIVE, I THINK I SHOULD DO IT FOR THE MILLIONS OF UNBORN - NO THAT'S NOT WHAT I'M THINKING ABOUT - I MEAN UNCONCEIVED KIDS WHO SHOULD HAVE A CHANCE TO BE A HUMAN BEING FOR A WHILE. ASSUMING THAT SOMEDAY I REALLY WILL GET RID OF THIS DISGUST ABOUT THE PROCESS OF MAKING A BABY, SOME OF THOSE KIDS I'M THINKING ABOUT COULD BE MY GRAND AND GREAT GRAND KIDS. IT'S LIKE A LITTLE PART OF ME WON'T GET A CHANCE TO BE REBORN AND BE A PERSON AGAIN AND AGAIN IF MANKIND GOES EXTINCT.
    I SUSPECT EXTINCTION COULD COME ABOUT IN AT LEAST TWO WAYS. ONE WOULD BE THAT WE HUMANS EVENTUALLY KILL EACH OTHER OFF AND ANOTHER WOULD BE THAT SOME DISEASE DOES US IN. MAYBE ANOTHER ICE AGE, BUT THAT WOULD COME ON GRADUALLY AND WE ARE PLENTY SMART ENOUGH TO PREPARE FOR THAT WITH WARM PLACES INSIDE TO LIVE AND GROW THINGS. MAYBE A COMET OR ASTEROID

COULD HIT THE EARTH AND MAKE LIFE IMPOSSIBLE. (WE PROBABLY SHOULD BE PLANNING ON BUILDING A HUGE GUN POWERFUL ENOUGH TO PULVERIZE IT WAY OUT IN SPACE.)

    WELL, SOME OF THOSE THINGS I CAN'T DO ANYTHING ABOUT BUT WE CAN ALL DECIDE TO LIVE IN SUCH A WAY THAT WE WILL NEVER KILL OURSELVES OFF. IT IS ANOTHER REASON TO LIVE ACCORDING TO POSITIVE VALUES THAT IMPROVE THINGS FOR PEOPLE. I THINK I AM DOING THAT PRETTY WELL. I KNOW A LOT OF PEOPLE AREN'T. IT'S PRETTY HARD TO KNOW HOW TO HELP THEM CHANGE. I WORRY ABOUT THAT. WE HAVE TO FIND WAYS OF GETTING ALONG AND BEING HELPFUL TO EACH OTHER. WE JUST HAVE TO AND IF HISTORY CAN BE BELIEVED, IT WON'T BE RELIGIONS THAT WILL HELP US DO IT. THEY SEEM TO HAVE BEEN THE WORST OFFENDERS OF ALL. WE ALL HAVE TO UNDERSTAND HOW DEAR HUMANITY IS AND MAKE IT OUR GOAL TO BE SURE IT IS SAVED TO GO ON AND ON FOREVER (WELL, <u>FOREVER</u> IS ANOTHER TOPIC I DO WANT TO TALK ABOUT, BUT NOT NOW.) GOODNIGHT

AGE 8 [GRADE 7]
    DI - OUR ENGLISH ASSIGNMENT IS TO WRITE AN ESSAY ABOUT THE THING THAT MEANS THE MOST TO US. I THOUGHT ABOUT IT A LONG TIME. MY FRANKLIN FAMILY WAS ONE OF THE TOP CONTENDERS. SO WAS MY SWIMMING SKILL - I WAS THE BEST 7 YEAR-OLD IN THE COUNTY MEET LAST SUMMER. BUT, I DECIDED TO WRITE ABOUT THE PART MOM AND POP AND I PLAY IN IMPROVING WHAT PARSON CALLS 'THE HUMAN CONDITION' - THAT HAS TO BE THE MOST PRECIOUS THING IN MY LIFE. WHEN PEOPLE ARE SICK OR HURT OR DOWN ON THEIR LUCK WE FRANKLINS ARE ALWAYS RIGHT THERE TO DO WHAT WE CAN. EVERY WEEK I VISIT THE KIDS OUT AT THE COUNTY HOME - THEY ARE ORPHANS AND LIVE WITH A BUNCH OF OLD PEOPLE. [LITTLE DID I RECOGNIZE THAT THOSE SAME PARAMETERS ALSO FIT ME IN MY SITUATION!] DOC AND I

SORT OF TEAM UP TO MAKE THEIR LIVES BETTER. ALSO, I MEET OLD MR. DEETS AT THE GROCERY STORE EVERY WEDNESDAY AFTER SCHOOL WITH MY WAGON TO TAKE HIS SACKS HOME FOR HIM. WE HAVE THIS THING WE DO. AFTER I'VE HELPED HIM PUT EVERY THING AWAY IN HIS KITCHEN, HE HOLDS OUT TWO PENNIES FOR ME IN HIS PALM AND I CLOSE HIS FINGERS OVER THEM AND SAY, "PUT THEM IN THE COLLECTION PLATE." HE SMILES AND NODS AND I AM SURE HE DOES PUT THEM IN. I LIKE MR. DEETS - HE MUST BE IN HIS 80S - HE'S NOT VERY SMART - DOC SAYS HE IS MENTALLY RETARDED - BUT IS ONE OF THE NICEST PEOPLE I HAVE PERSONALLY EVER MET AND I BELIEVE 'NICE' BEATS 'SMART' EVERY SINGLE TIME. WELL, I JUST HAVE TO MAKE SURE IT [THE ESSAY] DOESN'T SOUND LIKE I AM BRAGGING BECAUSE THAT IS NOT WHAT I MEAN. SHE SAID TO WRITE ABOUT WHAT IS MOST IMPORTANT TO ME AND PEOPLE'S WELL-BEING IS MOST IMPORTANT TO ME. MOST OF THE BOYS ARE WRITING ABOUT THEIR BIKES AND THE GIRLS ABOUT THEIR CLOTHES. I DON'T UNDERSTAND HOW THOSE THINGS COULD EVER BE MOST IMPORTANT IN ALL OF ONE'S LIFE. I GUESS I STILL HAVE A LOT TO LEARN ABOUT WHAT MAKES PEOPLE TICK. I WONDER WHAT MOM AND POP WOULD HAVE WRITTEN ABOUT. I GUESS I KNOW. IT WOULD HAVE BEEN THE SAME THING, BUT I AM SURE THEIR LOVE FOR ME WOULD HAVE JUST ABOUT TIED FOR FIRST PLACE. WE ARE REALLY LUCKY TO BE A PART OF THIS FAMILY, DI. (THERE SHOULD BE A BETTER WORD THAN LUCK OR FORTUNATE BECAUSE THEY DON'T REALLY SAY WHAT I FEEL.) . . .

POSITIVE, SOCIAL, AGREEMENT # 3

I WILL embrace and act upon positive values and goals that will tend to protect and enhance the human condition and this planet now and in the future,

RATHER THAN acting out of destructive self-interest for personal gain today, at the ultimate expense of humanity and the planet on which we live,

BECAUSE we each have but one brief moment in time to experience being this most marvelous of all creatures – a person – and when one of us is disallowed his or her opportunity to grow himself in all possible positive human dimensions, we are all diminished.

Topic Four:
Judging your own and others self-worth on the basis of their positive values and goals

AGE 7 [GRADE 4]

DI,

I'M CUTE AS A BUG (A <u>CUTE</u> BUG, I ASSUME). EVERYBODY SAYS SO. I KNOW THAT SOMEDAY I'LL GROW OUT OF CUTE AND INTO SOMETHING ELSE - MAYBE HANDSOME, MAYBE PLAIN, MAYBE UGLY (THOUGH I'M TOLD MY PARENTS WERE PRETTY GOOD LOOKING AND THAT SHOULD COUNT FOR SOMETHING). MRS HENRY ALWAYS SAYS TO MOM, "HE'S SO CUTE! I JUST LOVE HIM." I'M GLAD SHE LOVES ME, BUT I'D RATHER SHE'D LOVE ME BECAUSE I'M A REALLY GOOD HUMAN BEING. SHE NEVER BRINGS THAT UP.

MR. DEETS ALWAYS TELLS POP, "CRAIGY'S A PLEASURE TO HAVE AROUND - HE'S A REALLY GOOD KID AND ALWAYS MAKES ME LAUGH." I LIKE TO BE LIKED FOR THOSE REASONS. IT'S ABOUT THE REAL ME INSIDE THAT I'LL CARRY ALONG WITH ME FROM CUTE TO WHATEVER COMES LATER. TAKE GINNY (WELL, NO, DON'T TAKE HER. SHE'S MY BEST FRIEND. I DON'T LIKE TO THINK ABOUT WHEN WE GROW UP AND MOVE AWAY FROM EACH OTHER.) ANYWAY, I'LL START OVER. <u>CONSIDER</u> GINNY. SHE IS REALLY CUTE, REALLY SMART, AND REALLY KIND AND NICE, BUT WHEN I THINK ABOUT HER - THE REAL GINNY - IT'S JUST THAT'S SHE'S A NICE PERSON THAT I THINK ABOUT. PARSON'S WIFE PATS ME ON THE HEAD (I HATE THAT!!) AND SAYS, "HE'S SHARP AS A TACK, THAT LAD." (AS IF, EITHER MOM OR I HAD ANYTHING TO DO WITH THAT). I HATE BEING LIKED JUST BECAUSE I'M SMART. NEXT TO JUST BEING SO SMART IN THE FIRST PLACE, THAT'S THE THING I HATE THE MOST ABOUT IT. IT'S LIKE PEOPLE CAN'T (OR WON'T) LOOK BEYOND MY BRAIN AND

SEE THE REALLY NICE ME. I GUESS THAT'S WHY I WORK SO HARD AT IT. I'LL TELL YOU, DI, SOME DAYS IT'S JUST PLAIN EXHAUSTING TO BE SO NICE. BY NIGHT, MY SMILEY CHEEKS ACHE AND FEEL LIKE THEY'VE TURNED TO WELL-STRETCHED RUBBER. DON'T GET ME WRONG. I _WANT_ TO BE A NICE AND HELPFUL GUY. I JUST WISH PEOPLE DIDN'T LET THINGS LIKE LOOKS AND SMARTS GET IN THE WAY OF SEEING THAT. (SIGH!!!!) GOODNIGHT. LET'S HOPE MY CHEEKS RECUPERATE BY MORNING.

AGE 9 ½ [GRADE 9]

THE STATE SOCIAL WORKER JUST LEFT. ONE OF THEM COMES HERE EVERY YEAR TO LOOK OUT FOR MY WELFARE. I GUESS I'VE REALLY NEVER BEEN ADOPTED BY MOM AND POP - IT'S JUST BEEN AN ARRANGEMENT BETWEEN THEM, THE CITY FATHERS, AND THE COUNTY JUDGE. THAT'S OKAY. I'D SURE RATHER BE HERE THEN ANYWHERE ELSE. AS FAR AS I'M CONCERNED, THEY ARE MY PARENTS AND I AM A FRANKLIN. I ASKED THE SOCIAL WORKER WHY MOM AND POP NEVER ADOPTED ME. SHE SAID THE LAWS PROHIBITED IT. "BECAUSE THEY ARE TOO OLD, I GUESS?" I ASKED HER, FIGURING THAT HAD TO BE THE REASON. "NO, BECAUSE THEY ARE NEGRO. A NEGRO COUPLE CAN'T ADOPT A WHITE CHILD." "IF I WERE GREEN, COULD THEY ADOPT ME, 'CAUSE I'D BE WILLING TO DYE MY SKIN." WELL, THAT CONVERSATION WENT NOWHERE FAST. CLEARLY, THERE WERE THINGS THE LAWMAKERS FELT WERE MORE IMPORTANT THAN BEING LOVING, HELPFUL, CARING, UPRIGHT PEOPLE. I'LL LOOK INTO ALL THAT LATER ON.

EVERY YEAR IT'S A DIFFERENT LADY THAT COMES. I SUSPECT THAT'S BECAUSE MOM DOES SUCH A NUMBER ON EACH ONE THEY ALL REFUSE TO RETURN. WHILE THEY HAVE THEIR "PRIVATE" TALK, I'M SENT UP TO MY ROOM - AS IF ANYTHING CAN BE PRIVATE IN THIS LITTLE, FOUR

ROOM HOUSE. I PLAY ALONG AND JUST LISTEN AT THE FLOOR VENT. I CAN SEE PRETTY WELL FROM THERE, TOO. IT'S ALWAYS THE SAME DISCUSSION. THE SOCIAL WORKER SAYS, "I JUST DON'T THINK THESE SURROUNDINGS ARE FIT FOR SUCH A BOY."

MOM SAYS, "YOU MEAN THEY AREN'T CLEAN ENOUGH?"

"NO."

"NOT WARM ENOUGH?"

"NO."

"UNSAFE?"

"NO."

"I DON'T UNDERSTAND, I GUESS," MOM SAYS, LOOKING PUZZLED AND LEANING SLIGHTLY TOWARD THE LADY AS IF EXPECTING SOME HELPFUL EXPLANATION.

"WELL, HE HAS NO ADVANTAGES HERE THAT A BOY LIKE HIM NEEDS. YOU AND MR. FRANKLIN DIDN'T EVEN FINISH HIGH SCHOOL."

"TO BE COMPLETELY ACCURATE," MOM ALWAYS ADDS, "MR. FRANKLIN DIDN'T FINISH GRADE SCHOOL. YOU MAY WANT TO NOTE THAT IF YOUR INFORMATION IS INCORRECT."

"SEE!" THE SOCIAL WORKER SAYS.

"SEE?" MOMS ASKS, "SEE WHAT? SEE THAT HE HAS OVER 300 BOOKS IN HIS LIBRARY IN HIS ROOM - A PLACE YOU FOLKS NEVER EVEN ASK TO VISIT. SEE THAT AS A FAMILY WE READ A NEW BOOK TOGETHER AND DISCUSS IT EVERY WEEK - HAVE YOU READ <u>THE SUN ALSO RISES,</u> BUY THE WAY (SHE HOLDS IT UP) - THIS IS THE ONE WE'RE READING THIS WEEK. WE SEE THAT HE'S IN CHURCH EVERY SUNDAY MORNING AND EVERY WEDNESDAY EVENING. HE, LIKE HIS PARENTS, GIVES 20% OF WHAT HE

EARNS TO CHARITY - I SUPPOSE YOU DO THAT, TOO, THOUGH. EVERY SUNDAY AFTERNOON WE GO AS A FAMILY AND HELP SOME COMMUNITY MEMBER WHO'S IN NEED - CLEAN, COOK, WASH, GARDEN, REPAIR THINGS, MOW, SHOVEL - THINGS LIKE THAT. I ASSUME YOU UNDERSTAND FROM PERSONAL EXPERIENCE WHAT A WONDERFUL DIFFERENCE THAT CAN MAKE IN A BOYS OUTLOOK ON LIVING. WE LOVE THIS BOY - OUR SON - WITH ALL OUR HEARTS AND WE'D GLADLY GIVE UP OUR OWN LIVES FOR HIM IF NEED BE. ARE THOSE THE KINDS OF <u>DIS</u>ADVANTAGES YOU'RE CONCERNED ABOUT."

I CAN'T HELP BUT GIGGLE SO I GO BURY MY FACE IN MY PILLOW. MOM IS ALWAYS POLITE AND CALM AND CORDIAL, AND SMILES HER WONDERFUL SMILE THROUGH IT ALL.

"BUT THE JUNK IN THE BACK YARD." (IT'S AS IF WHEN ALL ELSE FAILS BRING THAT UP. <u>BIG MISTAKE!</u>)

"OH, YOU MEAN THE BICYCLE PARTS AND THE OLD WASHING MACHINE? CRAIGY AND POP ARE REBUILDING THE BIKES TO TAKE OUT TO THE CHILDREN AT THE COUNTY HOME. AND, CRAIGY HAS CONVERTED THE WASHING MACHINE INTO A PAPER SHREDDER AND FIRE PROOFER - I DON'T KNOW HOW IT WORKS - SO HE CAN MAKE INSULATION FROM OLD NEWSPAPERS FOR HOMES HERE IN SPRINGTOWN, SO WE CAN ALL CUT DOWN ON HEATING BILLS. YOU MUST COME BACK NEXT MONTH. HE'S ARRANGED TO GET A USED WINDMILL FROM A FARMER FOR ANOTHER ENERGY-SAVING PROJECT HE'S WORKING ON."

EVERY YEAR WHEN THE SOCIAL WORKER LEAVES OUR HOUSE, SHE SEEMS DAZED AND LOOKS DISHEVELED AND CONFUSED! SHE SEEMS TO WALK A STRAIGHT LINE ONLY WITH GREAT DIFFICULTY. LIKE I SAID, THE SAME ONE NEVER RETURNS AND NOBODY EVER COMES TO TAKE ME AWAY. WHAT WOULD POP AND I EVER WITHOUT MOM?

[Little did I understand, at nine, that an equally valid question would have been, "What would Mom and Pop have ever done without me?"]

I JUST THINK IT'S PRETTY SAD WHEN EVEN SOCIAL WORKERS BELIEVE THAT HAVING PARENTS WHO FINISHED SCHOOL AND ARE YOUR SAME COLOR IS MORE IMPORTANT THAN LIVING IN LOVE AND LEARNING TO BECOME AN ALTRUISTIC GUY FOR LIFE.

THE SOCIAL WORKER DID MAKE IT A POINT TO SEE MY ROOM - SHE HAD SOME DIFFICULTY CLIMBING THE LADDER TO GET UP HERE, WHICH STRUCK ME FUNNY. SHE LOOKED IN MY CLOSET AND DRESSER - A PRETTY RUDE THING TO DO WITHOUT ASKING PERMISSION IF YOU ASK ME - AND SHE COMMENTED THAT I ONLY HAD TWO SHIRTS AND TWO PAIRS OF JEANS AND HARDLY A WEEK'S WORTH OF UNDER WARE (THAT UNDER WARE THING WAS <u>REALLY</u> EMBARRASSING!). I ASKED HER WHY I'D NEED MORE THAN THAT. MOM WASHES AND IRONS EVERY DAY EXCEPT SUNDAY. I NEVER WAS ALLOWED TO LEAVE THE HOUSE IN DIRTY CLOTHES. WHY WOULD MORE BE BETTER? SHE DIDN'T ANSWER. I POINTED OUT TO HER THAT I HAD CHURCH PANTS AND SHIRT, BUT THEY WERE IN THE WASH. I SHOWED HER MY TIE BUT BY THEN, SHE SEEMED QUITE UNINTERESTED. SHE RAN HER FINGERS ACROSS MY BOOKS, TAKING OUT A FEW TO THUMB THROUGH THAT I'M SURE WERE WELL BEYOND HER MENTAL CAPABILITIES - EINSTEIN'S LIFE AND THOUGHT, TWO VOLUMES BY MARGARET MEADE, ONE BY RACHEL CARLSON, AND ONE OF MY FAVORITE WILLIAM JAMES BOOKS. IN ALL IT PRODUCED FIVE "HUMPHS" EACH ONE A BIT MORE PLEASANT SOUNDING THEN THOSE BEFORE I THOUGHT. BEST THING IS, DI, IT'S ALL OVER FOR ANOTHER YEAR. (I GET THE IDEA MOM MAY JUST BE A LITTLE PROUDER OF HERSELF THAN PARSON WOULD THINK IS APPROPRIATE! AFTER IT'S OVER, POP ALWAYS GIVES HER WHAT I ASSUME IS A PASSIONATE KISS. IT TAKES A PRETTY LONG TIME TO

RUN ITS COURSE. IT'S NEVER IN FRONT OF ME, OF COURSE - IT'S UNDER ME THROUGH THE VENT! HA! HA!) THEY SURE DO LOVE EACH OTHER.

AGE 9 ½ [GRADE 9]

DEAR DI,

    LOTS OF KIDS AND EVEN SOME ADULTS ARE NOT VERY NICE TO PETEY. (YOU REMEMBER HIM, DI - SIX AND REALLY SLOW IN THE BRAIN DEPARTMENT.) DOC SAYS HE WAS A BREECH BIRTH AND HAD THE CORD WRAPPED AROUND HIS NECK. A REGULAR BIRTH IS REVOLTING ENOUGH TO THINK ABOUT LET ALONE THAT KIND. ANYWAY, I LIKE PETEY. HE'S A GOOD LITTLE KID. HE SMILES A LOT AND HE TRIES TO BE HELPFUL - HE JUST DOESN'T KNOW HOW TO DO LOTS OF THE STUFF HE WANTS TO HELP WITH AND HE SEEMS TO HAVE CLUMSINESS BUILT RIGHT INTO HIS LITTLE BEING. WHEN HE STUMBLES OR LETS THE BALL HIT HIM IN THE FACE OR GETS BAD GRADES, THE OTHER KIDS LAUGH AT HIM. THAT REALLY HURTS ME. SINCE IT'S ABOUT THE ONLY WAY PETEY EVER GETS ANY ATTENTION, HE GOES ALONG WITH IT AND LAUGHS WITH THEM. I THINK SINCE HE'S SO DUMB (NO OFFENSE INTENDED) LOT S OF THAT GOES OVER HIS HEAD AND HE DOESN'T FEEL PUT DOWN - THAT'S LIKE A BLESSING, I GUESS.

    I GET A LOT OF THAT, TOO, BUT I HAVE TAKEN ON ELEANOR ROOSEVELT'S APPROACH TO IT. SHE SAYS YOU CAN NEVER BE PUT DOWN BY SOMEONE'S UGLY COMMENT UNLESS <u>YOU</u> ACCEPT IT AS THE TRUTH. SO, I JUST REFUSE TO THINK BADLY ABOUT MYSELF ON THE BASIS OF WHAT OTHERS MAY SAY TO OR ABOUT ME. IF WHAT THEY SAY <u>IS</u> TRUE, I THINK ABOUT IT AND I'M APPRECIATIVE. IF IT'S NOT OR IF IT DOESN'T MATTER, I LET IT ROLL OFF. I DON'T ACCEPT IT. I DON'T LET IT BECOME PART OF MY REALITY ABOUT MYSELF.

LIKE IN P. E. CLASS (AND I STILL DON'T UNDERSTAND WHY THEY WON'T LET ME TAKE P. E. WITH THE 4TH GRADE BOYS, MY AGE, INSTEAD OF MY FELLOW 9TH GRADERS). I CAN'T POSSIBLY DO SPORTS AS WELL AS THE 14 YEAR OLD GUYS - I'M TOO SHORT AND TOO LIGHT AND JUST NOT AS GOOD. THEY'VE HAD FIVE MORE YEARS TO PRACTICE. THEY MAKE FUN OF ME, BUT THEY DON'T SEEM TO REALIZE (OR CARE) THAT THEY ARE MAKING FUN OF ME FOR JUST BEING A NORMAL 9 ½ YEAR OLD, SO IT'S <u>THEIR</u> PROBLEM NOT <u>MINE</u>. IT ISN'T PLEASANT SEEING THEM MAKE SUCH FOOLS OF THEMSELVES BUT I JUST CHUCKLE INSIDE MY HEAD AT THEM (I LEARNED <u>QUICKLY</u> NOT TO CHUCKLE AT THEM <u>OUT</u>SIDE MY HEAD!!!).

AFTER P. E. WE HAVE TO TAKE SHOWERS AND THEY MAKE FUN OF MY 9 ½ YEAR OLD BODY. THEY PRETEND TO MISTAKE ME FOR A GIRL AND <u>THEN</u> SAY, "OH, NO, I GUESS THERE IS THE WORLDS' TINNIEST PETER THERE BETWEEN YOUR LEGS. GET THE MAGNIFYING GLASS GUYS AND WE'LL MAKE SURE." I JUST SMILE AND IGNORE THEM. COMPARED TO THEIR BIG, HAIRY, DANGLING, APPARATUSES, MINE DOES MORE RESEMBLE A WELL USED PENCIL STUB, BUT THAT'S HOW JOHN'S AND BILLY'S LOOK TOO, SO I'M QUITE SURE I'M DOING VERY WELL FOR A 9 ½ YEAR OLD BOY IN THE PENIS DEPARTMENT.

SPEAKING OF JOHN AND BILLY, WE'RE GOING SWIMMING AT THE CREEK LATER. IT WILL SURE BE GOOD TO BE NAKED WITH GUYS MY OWN AGE - WELL, THAT DIDN'T COME OUT SOUNDING EXACTLY LIKE I INTENDED, BUT I GUESS THERE'S NO NEED TO EXPLAIN HERE, IS THERE?

POSITIVE, SOCIAL, AGREEMENT # 4

I WILL define my self-worth in terms of my positive traits and values, my daily helpfulness to my fellow man, and the development of my own positive human potentials,

RATHER THAN in terms of the amount and kinds of stuff and status I accumulate or the power I can yield over others,

BECAUSE the good and helpful person who I am, deep down inside, is more important than what I have or how people look upon me. Of all the known species in the universe, only man possesses the positive potentials of love, compassion, rational problem solving, and planning for the welfare of future generations. So, to fail to live up these unique, positive potentials defines one as behaving well below his human capacities and more on the level of the lower animal species.

Topic Five:
Basing one's life on positive values

AGE 6 ½   [Grade 3]

    I HAD A LONG DISCUSSION WITH PRINCIPAL MARTIN TODAY . . .[ONE OF THE THINGS] WE TALKED ABOUT WAS THE RULES AT SCHOOL - I WAS <u>AGAINST</u> THEM AND HE WAS <u>FOR</u> THEM IN CASE YOU ARE WONDERING, DI. I GUESS THAT'S REALLY NOT RIGHT EITHER. WHAT THE RULES ARE TRYING TO DO IS MOSTLY OKAY, B UT THEY ARE ALL "DO <u>NOTS</u>". I POINTED OUT THAT I COULD SIT IN SCHOOL ALL DAY LONG AND ABIDE BY EVERY SINGLE RULE AND DO NOTHING AT ALL. "DO NOT SPIT. DO NOT TALK. DO NOT SQUIRM. DO NOT HIT. DO NOT GET OUT OF LINE. DO NOT SWEAR. DO NOT TATTLE. DO NOT ANSWER WITHOUT RAISING YOUR HAND. ETC, ETC."

    THE PROBLEM WITH "DO NOT" RULES IS THAT THEY NEVER TELL KIDS WHAT THEY <u>SHOULD</u> DO INSTEAD. MY SUGGESTION WAS THAT HE REPLACE ALL THE RULES WITH JUST ONE - "BE NICE". THAT WAY, IF YOU FOLLOWED THAT RULE YOU'D NEVER BREAK ANY OF THE "DO NOTS" AND IT GIVES A KID SOMETHING GOOD TO SHOOT FOR, YOU KNOW - <u>TO BE NICE!</u>

    HE PATTED ME ON THE HEAD (I HATE THAT!) AND SAID THAT MIGHT WORK FOR ME BUT MOST KIDS WEREN'T SMART ENOUGH FOR THAT TO WORK. I HATE THAT WHEN PEOPLE USE MY SMARTS AS A WEAPON AGAINST MY IDEAS. I WAS STEAMED, SO I FOLDED MY ARMS AND TURNED AWAY FROM HIM. HE PICKED ME UP IN THE CHAIR AND MOVED ME TO THE TABLE IN THE CORNER OF HIS OFFICE - IT HAS SORT OF BECOME MY OFFICE AWAY FROM THE CLASSROOM. HE PULLED THREE BOOKS OFF HIS SHELF AT RANDOM, PUT THEM ON THE TABLE, AND LEFT. INSTEAD OF RE-READING THE BOOKS, I MADE UP A SURVEY. AT THE TOP I WROTE: "IF A GROWN-UP TOLD YOU TO BE <u>NICE</u>, WHICH OF THESE THINGS WOULD YOU DO?" THEN I

LISTED 20 THINGS FROM THE "DO NOT" LIST - LIKE SWEAR, STEAL, TALK DURING CLASS, PASS NOTES - STUFF LIKE THAT - AND THEN MIXED INTO THE LIST 20 POSITIVE THINGS LIKE HELP CLEAN THE ERASERS AFTER SCHOOL, HOLD THE DOOR OPEN FOR TEACHERS, CLEAN THE MUD OFF YOUR SHOES AFTER RECESS AND THINGS LIKE THAT. AFTER SCHOOL, I GAVE MY SURVEY TO SIXTEEN KIDS ON THE PLAYGROUND AND YOU KNOW WHAT, DI? YOU KNOW WHAT? ALL 16 GOT EVERY SINGLE ONE RIGHT - BY <u>RIGHT</u> I MEAN THEY CHOSE TO DO THE SOCIALLY GOOD AND NOT TO DO THE SOCIALLY BAD THINGS. KIDS KNOW WHAT IT MEANS TO BE NICE - IT DOESN'T TAKE A FREAKISH, OVERGROWN BRAIN LIKE MINE TO KNOW WHAT IS AND ISN'T NICE.

WELL, YOU CAN BET I'LL MARCH THESE RESULTS INTO PRINCIPAL MARTIN FIRST THING MONDAY MORNING. HE'LL HAVE TO CHANGE THINGS AFTER HE SEES WHAT I FOUND OUT

[I *did*, of course! He *didn't*, of course! And as I remember, all I received for my effort was a smiling, double-long session of hair ruffling – my how I *double hated* that!]

AGE 8   [GRADE 6]

DI - JOHN STAYED OVERNIGHT WITH ME. HIS PARENTS WENT TO A WEDDING IN INDIANAPOLIS. WHEN HE LEFT THIS MORNING HE TOLD ME MY HOUSE WAS THE MOST COMFORTABLE HOUSE IN TOWN. (HE MEANT 'HOME' NOT 'HOUSE' BUT I DIDN'T CORRECT HIM.) I ASKED HIM WHY. HE SAID HE DIDN'T KNOW BUT THAT HE ALWAYS FELT GOOD WHILE HE WAS HERE. I HAVE REFLECTED ON THAT SINCE HE LEFT. I THOUGHT ABOUT HIS HOME. IT IS FILLED WITH THINGS HE ISN'T ALLOWED TO DO. HERE, MOM WOULD SAY (AS WE LEFT TO GO CLIMB THE PEAR TREE, FOR EXAMPLE) "HAVE A GOOD TIME AND TAKE CARE OF EACH OTHER." HIS MOM WOULD SAY, "DON'T FALL OUT OF THE TREE AND HURT YOURSELVES!" OR "DON'T GET INTO TROUBLE, YOU HEAR?" I'VE BEEN IN EVERY

HOME IN TOWN, DI, AND I WILL SAY I AGREE WITH JOHN, MINE IS THE MOST COMFORTABLE ONE. I AM SUCH A LUCK BOY. (THANK YOU GOD, IF IN FACT YOU ARE REALLY OUT THERE AND IF IN FACT IF YOU ARE, YOU REALLY HAD ANYTHING TO DO WITH IT.)

POSITIVE, SOCIAL, AGREEMENT # 5

I WILL base my living style on Positive Values

RATHER THAN on negative values,

BECAUSE Positive Values tell me what to do, what to move toward, what and who to include, and provide a variety of acceptable action alternatives, while negative values tell people what not to do, what to keep away from, what and who to exclude, and prohibit without providing appropriate action alternatives.

Topic Six:
Regularly demonstrating one's positive values

AGE 7 [GRADE FOUR]

DI - I'VE DECIDED IT'S ONE THING TO HAVE GOOD INTENTIONS BUT IT'S A WHOLE OTHER THING TO ACT THEM OUT EVERY DAY. I KNOW GINNY'S DAD BELIEVES IN BEING A GOOD PERSON AND IN TAKING CARE OF THOSE IN NEED BUT HE ALWAYS HAS EXCUSES THAT KEEP HIM FROM FOLLOWING THROUGH. TODAY WAS CLEAN-UP-THE-CHURCH-SATURDAY FOR SEPTEMBER. HE SIGNED UP TO HELP WITH THE ROOFING OVER THE ANTEROOM (THAT MAY BE MISSPELLED - IT CAME OUT LOOKING LIKE A PLACE IN WHICH YOU'D PLAY POKER - NOT EXACTLY A CHURCHLY ACTIVITY.) (AND, GOD, IF YOU'RE WONDERING, I ONLY KNOW ABOUT POKER BECAUSE BILLY'S BIG BROTHER TALKS ABOUT IT.) ANYWAY, MR. ROBERTS DIDN'T SHOW UP TO HELP. IT WAS EMBARRASSING FOR HIS FAMILY AND SURE NOT HELPFUL FOR THE CHURCH. SO YOU SEE, GOOD INTENTIONS AREN'T WORTH THE GRAY MATTER THEY'RE STORED IN (OR ON?) UNLESS THEY ARE ACTED ON. LOTS OF (WELL, SOME, ANYWAY) PEOPLE WHO GO TO CHURCH EVERY SUNDAY REALLY AREN'T VERY NICE PEOPLE. I WONDER IF THEY JUST GO FOR SHOW AND DON'T BELIEVE IN WHAT THE CHURCH TEACHES, OR IF THEY ARE LIKE MR. ROBERTS AND THEY DO BELIEVE BUT THEY CAN'T MAKE THEMSELVES DEMONSTRATE THOSE BELIEFS IN THEIR DAILY LIFE? I WONDER WHY I WONDER ABOUT STUFF LIKE THIS. OTHER KIDS DON'T SEEM TO. SOMETIMES I WISH I DIDN'T EITHER. I LIKE QUESTIONS WITH VERIFIABLE ANSWERS. GOOD NIGHT.

AGE 9 [GRADE EIGHT]

VALUES HELD BUT NOT ACTED ON ARE LIKE NO VALUES AT ALL. DOC CALLS IT "LIP SERVICE." IT'S LIKE LYING TO YOURSELF - SAYING YOU BELIEVE IN SOME

REALLY GOOD GOAL OR VALUE BUT NEVER (OR SELDOM) GETTING AROUND TO LIVING BY IT. WE JUST FINISHED THE COMMUNITY CHEST DRIVE (AND JUST FOR THE RECORD I <u>DID</u> ONCE AGAIN BRING IN THE MOST CONTRIBUTIONS - THANK YOU!) PEOPLE WONDER HOW I DO IT EVERY YEAR. I'LL TELL YOU HOW I DO IT, DI. THE PEOPLE ON THE HILL ARE THE BIGGEST "VALUE LIARS" I KNOW. I DON'T MEAN THEY ARE BAD PEOPLE - I DON'T THINK THEY ARE. BUT THEY KNOW THEY ACTUALLY CONTRIBUTE VERY LITTLE TO THE GOOD OF OUR LITTLE TOWN - EXCEPT THE MAYOR, I SUPPOSE - ANYWAY, I USE THAT VALUE-LIE-THING TO THE ADVANTAGE OF THE COMMUNITY CHEST. I KNOCK ON THEIR DOOR AND SAY, "I KNOW HOW BUSY YOU FOLKS ARE, SO YOU CAN'T CONTRIBUTE MUCH TIME TO HELP OUT OUR TOWN, SO I WANTED TO MAKE SURE YOU HAD A CHANCE TO SUPPORT OUR COMMUNITY CHEST WITH A MONEY DONATION." WHEN THEY HAND ME A FIVE-DOLLAR BILL (OR WHATEVER SIZE) I LOOK IT OVER AND THEN LOOK UP AT THEM WITH A FURROWED BROW. THEY ALMOST ALWAYS DOUBLE IT ON THE SPOT. I THINK IT'S USING THEIR GUILT FEELINGS - BETTER STILL I THINK I'M GIVING THEM AN OPPORTUNITY TO EASE THEIR GUILT FEELINGS. I HOPE THEY FEEL GOOD ABOUT THEIR DONATION. (BY THE WAY, MY SECRET METHOD IS JUST BETWEEN YOU AND ME, DI.) THEN TAKE DOC, FOR EXAMPLE. HE'S AS HARDHEADED AND OPINIONATED A MAN AS EVER LIVED, BUT WHEN HE SAYS HE BELIEVES IN SOMETHING YOU CAN BE SURE THAT'S HOW HE LIVES. HE IS HELPFUL AND COMPASSIONATE (THOUGH HE WORKS HARD AT HIDING THAT FOR SOME REASON) AND DOES LOTS OF WONDERFUL THINGS FOR PEOPLE IN THIS AREA THAT NOBODY EVER EVEN KNOWS ABOUT (WELL, EXCEPT ME. THERE'S NOTHING THAT GOES ON AROUND HERE THAT I DON'T KNOW ABOUT. IT'S AMAZING WHAT YOU LEARN BY DROPPING IN ON A HALF-DOZEN BREAKFAST TABLES EVERY MORNING!) I GUESS I WAS GETTING TO A

BOTHERSOME THING ABOUT DOC. HE IS ONE OF THE FINEST MEN WHO EVER TROD THIS EARTH AND YET HE DOESN'T BELIEVE IN GOD. HE'S HONEST AND OPEN ABOUT IT. BUT EVEN SO, HE HAS HIS LIST OF POSITIVE PRINCIPLES (WHICH HE CAN STATE - I'VE ASKED HIM TO DO THAT) AND HE LIVES BY THEM EVERY DAY. IT'S LIKE PARSON'S A GOOD MAN (AND HE IS A VERY GOOD MAN) BUT HE'S THAT WAY BECAUSE HE'S AFRAID OF GOD, WHILE DOC IS A GOOD MAN BECAUSE HE LOVES HIS FELLOW MAN SO VERY MUCH. I'M AFRAID I'M LEANING MORE AND MORE TOWARD DOC'S POINT OF VIEW. THAT WILL BREAK MOM AND POP'S HEART. PERHAPS I DON'T NEED TO BE OPEN ABOUT THAT SO LONG AS I LIVE A GOOD AND HELPFUL LIFE. I SURE WISH I WERE A LOT DUMBER THAN I AM, DI. BEING SMART MAKES BEING A KID VERY, VERY DIFFICULT (AND OFTEN, LIKE JUST NOW, VERY, VERY, SCARY.)

POSITIVE, SOCIAL, AGREEMENT # 6

I WILL not only base my life on positive, humanity-friendly values but each day I will act on them

RATHER THAN merely subscribing to positive values without regularly acting on them

BECAUSE positive change does not take place through belief alone, but through action based on positive beliefs.

Positive Vision + Positive Value + Positive Action = Positive Contribution
    (GOAL)   (GUIDE)   (BEHAVIOR)   (IMPROVED HUMAN
                                                                             CONDITION)

Topic Seven:
Emphasizing cooperation in one's life

AGE 9 [GRADE 8]

GEEZE, DI! (SORRY FOR SWEARING.) I TRY TO DO WHAT'S RIGHT AND I STILL GET INTO TROUBLE. MRS. TRUMBLE, MY READING TEACHER (AND WHY WE STILL HAVE READING IN THE 8TH GRADE IS BEYOND ME!) DID THIS 'READING RACE' THING THIS MONTH. FOR EVERY BOOK YOU READ YOU WRITE A ONE PAGE REPORT AND SHE TACKS IT ON A CHART. THE ONE WHO READS THE MOST WILL 'WIN' THE RACE. (WHOOPEE!) I READ LOTS OF BOOKS I DIDN'T TELL HER ABOUT. I THOUGHT ELLEN KAY SHOULD WIN BECAUSE SHE READS A LOT AND SHE'S REALLY SMART AND I JUST THOUGHT SHE SHOULD HAVE A CHANCE TO WIN. WELL, TRUMBLE FOUND OUT AND SAID IT WAS LIKE LYING. SO, SHE MADE ME LIST ALL MY BOOKS. IT WAS THE DARNDEST (SORRY, AGAIN) THING. SHE PUNISHED ME BY MAKING ME WIN. IT'S A STRANGE WORLD, I'LL TELL YOU THAT, DI.

AGE 9 ½ [GRADE 9]

. . . COMPETITION!!! I JUST DON'T UNDERSTAND WHY EVERYBODY THINKS IT IS SO GREAT. AS FAR AS I CAN SEE, EVERYTHING ABOUT IT IS DESTRUCTIVE. ALMOST EVERYBODY ALWAYS LOSES - ONLY ONE CAN WIN - SO ALL THE LOSERS FEEL BAD AND THEN THE GUY WHO WINS HAS TO WORK EVEN HARDER TO STAY THE BEST AND LIVES BEING AFRAID HE MAY BE BEAT THE NEXT TIME SO HE CAN'T EVEN REALLY ENJOY HIS VICTORY. . . . I WONDER IF THERE IS 'SLEEPING' COMPETITION - I BETTER NOT MENTION IT OR THERE <u>WILL</u> BE. GOOD NIGHT. GRRRRRR

AGE 9 ½ [GRADE 9]

WELL, DI, YOU KNOW I HAVE THIS PROBLEM ABOUT COMPETITIVE THINGS. SO, I INVENTED A COUPLE OF BOARD GAMES THAT ARE BASED ON COOPERATION BETWEEN THE TWO PLAYERS. THEY TRY TO IMPROVE

THEIR COMBINED SCORE FROM GAME TO GAME BY HELPING EACH OTHER. ALL THE KIDS LIKE THEM - ESPECIALLY DOMINECKERS, BUT YOU KNOW WHAT? THREE DAYS LATER, THEY HAD DIVIDED THEMSELVES INTO TWO-MAN TEAMS AND WERE COMPARING SCORES AMONG TEAMS TO SEE WHO WAS THE BEST TEAM. IT'S LIKE A DEATH WISH, DI. I GIVE THEM A WAY SO EVERYBODY CAN FEEL GOOD ABOUT THEMSELVES EVERY TIME THEY PLAY AND THEY CHANGE IT BACK INTO A 'LET'S SEE HOW WE CAN CHANGE THIS GAME SO MOST OF US CAN FEEL BAD ABOUT THE RESULTS'. PERHAPS IT'S ALL ABOUT EXPECTATIONS THEY HAVE BEEN TAUGHT BY ADULTS. I'D SAY IT WAS IN THE HUMAN GENE POOL EXCEPT MOM, POP AND I AREN'T THAT WAY (AND WE ARE CLEARLY NOT BLOOD RELATIVES) - NEITHER IS GINNY, ACTUALLY, THOUGH HER OLDER BROTHERS SURE ARE. IT JUST SEEMS A SHAME PEOPLE THINK THEY HAVE TO BE THE BEST AT SOMETHING IN ORDER TO FEEL GOOD ABOUT THEMSELVES. THEY MISS OUT ON ENJOYING THE PROCESS. I PERSONALLY ENJOY BASKETBALL A LOT EVEN THOUGH I'M WAY TOO SHORT AND SMALL TO REALLY DO WELL AGAINST THE OTHER GUYS. THE POINT IS, I DON'T CARE IF I WIN (GOOD THING SINCE I NEVER DO). I JUST LOVE TO PLAY THE GAME. IT'S THE SAME WITH MARBLES - I'LL ALWAYS TAKE THE DIFFICULT SHOT OVER THE EASY ONE JUST BECAUSE IT'S MORE OF A CHALLENGE. I LOSE LOTS OF MARBLES THAT WAY BUT THAT'S NOT THE IMPORTANT PART TO ME. SOMEHOW, IF I AM EVER GOING TO SAVE THIS WORLD - I HAVE TO FIND A WAY TO MAKE 'COOPERATION' - WHERE EVERYBODY WINS AND FEELS GOOD ABOUT THEMSELVES - MORE IMPORTANT THAN COMPETITION. (<u>I COULD USE A LITTLE HELP HERE, GOD!</u>)

POSITIVE, SOCIAL, AGREEMENT # 7

I WILL base my living style largely on cooperation

RATHER THAN largely on competition,

BECAUSE with cooperation most folks win and it emphasizes the equality of worth among all people,
While with competition, most folks lose (there being only one winner) and it emphasizes perfection as the necessary component in self-worth.

Topic Eight:
Maintaining an altruistic focus

AGE 6 [GRADE TWO]

I EARNED 20 CENTS THIS AFTERNOON FOR HELPING MRS. GOLDSMITH CLEAN OUT THEIR BASEMENT. THAT MEANT I COULD SPEND A NICKEL ON A BABY RUTH BAR (I CLEARED IT WITH MOM AHEAD OF TIME). MARK BROWN WAS HANGING AROUND THE STORE - HE'S MY AGE AND SOMETIMES WE DO STUFF TOGETHER THOUGH IN GENERAL HE WOULD RATHER MAKE FUN OF MY BRAIN THAN ENJOY MY COMPANY. ANYWAY, MARK SAW I HAD 15 CENTS LEFT AND ASKED WHY I DIDN'T BUY THREE MORE CANDY BARS. (I THINK HE HAD HIS EYE ON ONE OF THEM FOR HIMSELF.) I BROKE OFF A PIECE OF MINE FOR HIM AND WE WALKED TOGETHER 'TIL WE GOT TO HIS PLACE. I EXPLAINED TO HIM THAT IN MY HOME WE ALWAYS PUT 20% OF WHAT WE EARNED IN THE CHARITY JAR AND USED IT TO HELP OTHERS WHO WERE IN NEED AND THAT WE ALWAYS SAVED ANOTHER 10% FOR THINGS WE WOULD NEED OR WANT IN THE FUTURE. "ALTOGETHER THAT IS THREE CENTS OUT OF EVERY DIME," I EXPLAINED, SINCE MARK CLEARLY DIDN'T UNDERSTAND ABOUT PERCENTS. SO, OUT OF THIS 20 CENTS, THAT'S 4 CENTS FOR CHARITY, 2 CENTS FOR SAVINGS AND 5 CENTS FOR THE BABY RUTH. THAT'S 11 CENTS, WHICH MEANT THERE WAS ONLY 9 CENTS LEFT. AT MOST, I COULD BUY ONE MORE CANDY BAR. I DIDN'T TELL HIM THIS, BUT I'M SAVING THAT NICKEL TO BUY ONE ON SATURDAY FOR GINNY AND ME TO SHARE. I FELT BAD FOR HIM BECAUSE HE DIDN'T SEEM TO UNDERSTAND EITHER CHARITY OR SAVINGS. I HOPE HE CATCHES ONTO THE CONCEPTS PRETTY SOON OR IT WILL PROBABLY BE TOO LATE TO MAKE A PEOPLE-PERSON [THAT WAS MY OPPOSITE OF 'STUFF PERSON' AT SIX] OUT OF HIM.

[Mark grew up to be a Methodist minister and, of course, I take full credit for that, based upon our talk that Wednesday afternoon!]

AGE 8 ½ [GRADE SEVEN]

     DEAR DI - I JUST FINISHED MY SECOND BOOK, DI. - WELL, I THOUGHT OF IT AS A BOOK. IT TOOK UP 28 PAGES OF HANDWRITING. THEN, MRS. SHIPLEY, MR. MARTIN'S SECRETARY, TYPED IT UP FOR ME AND IT TURNED OUT TO BE JUST FOUR PAGES. AT FIRST I WAS DISAPPOINTED BUT THEN I REALIZED THAT I MUST BE A VERY GOOD WRITER TO MANAGE GETTING A WHOLE BOOK'S WORTH OF IDEAS INTO JUST FOUR PAGES. I TOOK THE PAGES FROM MRS. SHIPLEY DOWN TO JAKE WILSON, THE EDITOR OF THE CHRONICLE [Springtown's weekly, local, paper – eight pages during an especially newsworthy week!] HE SAID I COULD TYPE SET MY BOOKS THERE AND HE'D PRINT UP SOME COPIES FOR ME. HE SHOWED ME HOW TO TURN IT INTO 12 PAGES BY PRINTING TWO BOOK SIZE PAGES THE LONG WAY ACROSS A SHEET. SO, NOW I'M DOING THE TYPESETTING. YOU HAVE TO DO EVERY LINE BACKWARDS - RIGHT TO LEFT - SO WHEN IT PRINTS IT COMES OUT FRONTWARD. JAKE CAN SET A LINE IN 45 SECONDS. MY FIRST LINE TOOK ME FIVE MINUTES BUT I'LL GET THE HANG OF IT. I CHECK IT WITH A MIRROR SO I'M SURE I HAVEN'T MESSED UP. I'M GOING OVER FOR A HALF-HOUR BEFORE SCHOOL EVERY MORNING. BUT, I GOT OFF THE TRACK. IT IS A BOOK ABOUT ALTRUISM - THAT MEANS MAKING OTHER PEOPLE'S NEEDS AT LEAST AS IMPORTANT, IF NOT MORE IMPORTANT, THAN YOUR OWN. I FIND <u>THIS</u> THING QUITE INTERESTING, DI. MR. CRAMER LET ME OUT OF ENGLISH THE PAST THREE WEEKS (QUITE ALTRUISTIC!) SO I COULD GO TO MY TABLE IN MR. MARTIN'S OFFICE (ALTRUISTIC OF MR. MARTIN FOR PROVIDING IT) TO WRITE THE BOOK. MR. MARTIN LET MRS. SHIPLEY TYPE IT UP FOR ME (ALTRUISTIC OF BOTH OF THEM). JAKE IS LETTING ME USE HIS SHOP (ALTRUISTIC), AND DOC SAYS HE'LL CHIP IN UP TO $5.00 TO HELP PAY FOR THE PRINTING (ALTRUISTIC - I HAD TEN DOLLARS SAVED FOR IT, MYSELF.) THEN, I'M GOING TO GIVE THE BOOK AWAY TO THOSE I THINK NEED TO

LEARN ABOUT ALTRUISM (I'M STARTING OVER ON THE HILL.). ISN'T THAT A REMARKABLE SET OF EVENTS - ALL THAT ALTRUISTIC BEHAVIOR TO PUT OUT A BOOK ON ALTRUISM. I THINK THE WORD IS 'IRONY' - I'LL LOOK IT UP. I ACTUALLY MADE A BASKET IN P. E. TODAY. THE GUYS CARRIED ME AROUND ON THEIR SHOULDERS. I HAVE THE IDEA IT WAS AS MUCH MAKING FUN OF ME AS IT WAS CELEBRATING FOR ME. AT ANY RATE, IT FELT REALLY GOOD AND I LET MYSELF ENJOY IT. I THOUGHT MY CHEEKS WOULD BUST! POP GOT A BIG CHARGE OUT OF IT WHEN I TOLD HIM.

AGE 9 [GRADE NINE]

DI - GINNY'S FAMILY IS LIKE A MICROCOSM (I LOVE THAT WORD - JUST LEARNED IT BUT MAY HAVE MISSPELLED IT) OF SOCIAL INTERACTION TYPES. HER OLDEST BROTHER, TOM, IS A DESTROYER. HER DAD IS AN OBSERVER. HER MOTHER IS A PEOPLE USER - NOT TO A TERRIBLE DEGREE BUT STILL A PEOPLE USER, AND GINNY, IS A BUILDER. I THINK OUR RELATIONSHIP HAS HELPED EACH OTHER A LOT ALL THESE YEARS. WE'VE LEARNED FROM EACH OTHER. SHE'S LEARNED ABOUT ALL THE POSITIVE STUFF FROM MY FAMILY AND HER GOOD, COMMON SENSE HAS TENDED TO KEEP ME FROM DOING LOTS OF FOOLISH THINGS. WE THINK ALIKE ABOUT MOST THINGS. I CAN SEE SHE IS MATURING PHYSICALLY NOW - FROM THE WAIST UP, AT LEAST - I SURE HOPE THAT DOESN'T CHANGE THINGS BETWEEN US. ME, I'M STILL A LITTLE BOY BETWEEN MY LEGS. ON THE ONE HAND, I'M QUITE INTERESTED TO LEARN HOW MATURING EFFECTS THE WAY BOYS THINK AND ACT. ON THE OTHER HAND, I'VE NOT SEEN MUCH THAT IS SOCIALLY REDEEMING ABOUT ADOLESCENTS, SO I'M A BIT FRIGHTENED ABOUT THOSE CHANGES AS WELL. ANYWAY, GINNY AND I WORRY TOGETHER SOMETIMES ABOUT ALL THE SELFISHNESS WE SEE GOING ON AROUND US (AND ADOLESCENTS SEEM TO BE REALLY SELF-CENTERED, WHICH IS WHY I BROUGHT

THAT UP.). SO MANY PEOPLE CAN'T SEEM TO SEE BEYOND WHAT THEY WANT FOR THEMSELVES TO THE THINGS THAT ARE NEEDED BY OTHER PEOPLE. DURING THE WAR, I THINK PEOPLE WERE MORE PRONE TO BE MUTUALLY HELPFUL BUT NOW THAT IT'S OVER, IT'S LIKE IT'S EVERYBODY FOR HIMSELF. AND THAT, IT SEEMS TO US, IS THE ATTITUDE THAT STARTED THAT WAR IN THE FIRST PLACE. HOW CAN GROWN-UPS BE SO STUPID - ETERNALLY STUPID, IT SEEMS. (I LIKE THAT PHRASE - I HATE WHAT IT HAS TO SAY ABOUT OUR FUTURE.)

POSITIVE, SOCIAL, AGREEMENT # 8

I WILL altruistically keep my focus on the welfare of mankind (mindful that I am a member of that group) [humanity-centered]

RATHER THAN focusing primarily on myself to the exclusion of mankind as a whole [self-centered],

BECAUSE (1) Unless people take good care of each other the species will surely die out. (2) People who are well cared for (safe, happy, loved, productive, well-adjusted, self-esteemed) are easy to live among, while those who are not (ignored, needy, fearful, sad, angry and poorly adjusted) are very difficult (and very expensive) to live among.

Topic Nine:
Making the first move to resolve conflict

AGE 7 ½ [GRADE FIVE]
DEAR DIARY,

POP MADE AN IMPORTANT POINT TO ME TONIGHT. HE KNEW THAT BRENDA AND I HAD A FALLING OUT OVER DECORATING MY CLASSROOM FOR VALENTINES DAY. HE ASKED ME IF I HAD HANDLED THAT PROBLEM YET. I SAID I WOULD APOLOGIZE TO HER IF SHE WOULD APOLOGIZE TO ME FIRST. HE DIDN'T TELL ME WHAT TO DO BUT HERE IS WHAT HE SAID, DI. "UNRESOLVED PROBLEMS BETWEEN FOLKS CAN FESTER FOR A LIFETIME WASTING THE DAILY POSSIBILITY OF WONDERFUL TIMES AND REWARDING RELATIONSHIPS. IF EVERYONE WAITED FOR THE OTHER PERSON TO MAKE THE FIRST MOVE TOWARD A SOLUTION, SUCH PROBLEMS WOULD NEVER GET RESOLVED WOULD THEY?" (WELL, THOSE WERE ALMOST HIS VERY WORDS BUT THAT IS WHAT HE MEANT.) "BUT WHAT ABOUT THE UNFAIRNESS OF ME ALWAYS HAVING TO MAKE THE FIRST MOVE?" I SAID ABACK TO HIM. "PERHAPS YOU NEED TO CONSIDER FORGETTING ABOUT FAIR AND UNFAIR AND SEEING THESE TIMES AS GRAND OPPORTUNITIES TO WORK YOUR MAGIC AND SAVE A RELATIONSHIP." IT'S LIKE IF I TAKE THE FIRST STEP THEN I CAN SORT OF TAKE CREDIT (IN MY HEAD ONLY OF COURSE) FOR HAVING SOLVED THE PROBLEM AND OPENED UP THE POSSIBILITY FOR BETTER STUFF BETWEEN BRENDA AND ME. IF I WAIT, I'M THE ONE KEEPING THE DOOR CLOSED TO MY OWN HAPPINESS. W O W ! ! ! I SURE DO LOVE POP. I MEAN, I'D LOVE HIM EVEN IF HE WASN'T SO WISE. I'M JUST SO LUCKY TO HAVE HIM, SOMETIMES I CAN'T FIND WAYS BIG ENOUGH TO LET HIM KNOW. I WONDER IF HE WOULD COME TO MY CLASSROOM SOMETIMES AND JUST BE WISE FOR THE OTHER KIDS.

AGE 7 ½ [THE NEXT DAY}
DEAR DIARY,
      WELL, I TOLD BRENDA TODAY I COULD UNDERSTAND WHY SHE WANTED FRILLY VALENTINE DECORATIONS - HER BEING A GIRL AND ALL - AND THAT I THOUGHT SHE AND THE GIRLS SHOULD GO AHEAD AND DECORATE THAT WAY. I ALSO SAID THAT SINCE BOYS REALLY DIDN'T LIKE THE FRILLY FLOWERS AND BIRD STUFF, THAT I THOUGHT WE COULD DECORATE THE BACK OF THE ROOM WITH RACECARS AND HORSES. SHE ROLLED HER EYES BUT AGREED. SHE KISSED ME ON MY CHEEK. WHAT IS THIS WITH 5TH GRADE GIRLS AND KISSING?? EDDY WAS TELLING US GUYS HOW HE KISSED ELLEN KAY ON HER LIPS AND HOW THEY TOUCHED THE ENDS OF THEIR TONGUES TOGETHER. IF THAT ISN'T THE MOST REVOLTING THING I'VE EVER HEARD - WELL, ALMOST! BUT THAT'S ONLY A TINY PART OF THE PROBLEM, DI. I'M SMART ENOUGH TO KNOW THAT IN A FEW YEARS I AM PROBABLY GOING TO START WANTING TO DO THAT SAME DISGUSTING STUFF MYSELF. DOC SAYS I'LL UNDERSTAND ALL ABOUT IT ONCE THAT TIME COMES. THE BEST THING ABOUT IT IS THAT EVEN WITH MY MAMMOTH BRAIN, IT'S ONE THING I CAN'T UNDERSTAND RIGHT NOW. I LOVE THAT PART OF IT, YOU KNOW - SOMETHING I CAN'T POSSIBLY UNDERSTAND JUST WITH MY BRAIN. HALLELUIAH AND AMEN!!! ANYWAY, I TOOK THE FIRST STEP IN SOLVING THE PROBLEM WITH BRENDA. I KNOW SHE THINKS SHE "WON" BECAUSE I WENT FIRST, BUT THAT'S OKAY. I KNOW I REALLY WON BECAUSE I OPENED THE DOOR AND ALLOWED A SOLUTION TO HAPPEN. OOOXXX (SHUDDER, SHUDDER) HA! HA! HA! (THEY ACTUALLY TOUCHED TONGUES, DI!)

POSITIVE, SOCIAL, AGREEMENT # 9

I WILL make the first move to resolve conflict, misunderstanding or other interpersonal tension, and offer compromise where it is essential for the ultimate good of the species,

RATHER THAN demanding the other person always make the first move,

BECAUSE if no one ever makes the first move, conflicts and misunderstandings can never be resolved. Stated another way, if everyone waits for the other person to make the first move, that first move will never be made.

Topic Ten:
Maintaining a sense of humor about life and oneself

AGE 6 [GRADE TWO]
DEAR DIARY,
    I HAVE KNOWN FOR A LONG TIME THAT SOME FOLKS - LOTS OF FOLKS, REALLY, I GUESS - DON'T SEEM TO HAVE MUCH OF A SENSE OF HUMOR ABOUT THEMSELVES. THEY TAKE THEMSELVES WAY TO SERIOUSLY. IF THEY MAKE A MISTAKE THEY TRY TO COVER IT UP OR DENY IT LIKE IT MEANS THEY ARE NOT A WORTHY PERSON, OR SOMETHING. MANY OF THEM EVEN TRY TO BLAME SOMEBODY ELSE. TEACHERS SEEM ESPECIALLY AFFLICTED WITH THIS MALADY. (THAT WAS A GREAT SENTENCE!) MY FAMILY GETS A BIG KICK OUT OF OUR LITTLE FOIBLES. I SPILLED MY MILK AT SUPPER NOT LONG AGO AND MOM ASKED, "YOU ON MR. MILLER'S [THE DAIRY FARMER] PAYROLL, NOW, SON?" WE GIGGLED ABOUT IT LIKE GIRLS. WHEN POP PUT THE MONEY JAR [CHANGE SAVED FOR CHARITY] <u>IN</u> THE ICE BOX [NON-ELECTRIC REFRIGERATOR] INSTEAD OF <u>ON TOP</u> OF IT WHERE IT IS KEPT, HE JOKED SOMETHING ABOUT JUST WANTING TO HAVE SOME 'COLD CASH.' ONE SUNDAY MORNING MOM WAS IN A HURRY AND PUT ON ONE WHITE GLOVE AND ONE BLACK GLOVE [DRESS GLOVES, WHICH WOMEN WORE BACK THEN]. SHE LOOKED DOWN AT THEM AND SAID, "BLACK AND WHITE - THAT SEEMS APPROPRIATE FOR THIS GANG." [MY 'ADOPTIVE' PARENTS WERE AS BLACK AS I WAS LILY WHITE.] AT COMMUNION SUPPER AT CHURCH LOT LONG AGO I WAS SITTING WITH POP AT THE MEN'S TABLE, AND I SNEEZED, AND A LARGE BUGGER SHOT OUT OF MY NOSE AND INTO MY SOUP BOWL. POP QUIPPED, "SON, 'THAT<u>SNOT</u>' THE THING TO DO IN CHURCH." IT WAS THE ONLY TIME I CAN REMEMBER THE MEN'S TABLE LAUGHING DURING COMMUNION. (LATER, PARSON SAID HE SUSPECTED IT WAS POP AND MY DOING.) BUT MY POINT IS THAT I WAS WONDERING WHY PEOPLE ARE SO

SENSITIVE OR SERIOUS ABOUT THEMSELVES THAT THEY CAN'T ENJOY THINGS LIKE THAT. DOC SAYS THEY ARE DEFENSIVE BECAUSE THEY HAVE FRAGILE SELF-CONCEPTS - IT DOESN'T TAKE MUCH FOR THEM TO QUESTION THEIR OWN WORTH. SINCE PARSON IS GENERALLY HUMORLESS HIMSELF, I HAVEN'T ASKED HIS OPINION ON THE SUBJECT. IT'S MY IDEA THAT IF YOU LIKE YOURSELF AND KNOW YOU ARE OKAY, YOU CAN ENJOY YOUR OWN LITTLE MISTAKES. MORE THAN A FEW TIMES, I'VE BEEN SENT TO THE OFFICE FOR ENJOYING MINE A BIT TOO MUCH. I SUPPOSE THERE NEEDS TO BE SOME LIMITS ON WHERE AND HOW YOU DO IT. PRINCIPAL MARTIN - WHO HAS AN OPINION ABOUT EVERYTHING IN MY LIFE - SAYS HE THINKS I OVERDO MY MISTAKE CELEBRATIONS IN ORDER TO SHOW EVERYBODY I'M REALLY NOT ALWAYS RIGHT - NOT ALWAYS THE SMART GUY. I BELIEVE HE IS RIGHT THIS TIME. (IT DOESN'T KEEP ME FROM DOING IT, BUT I BELIEVE HE IS RIGHT!) MY FAMILY LOVES TO LAUGH. I'VE NOTICED THAT LAUGHING SEEMS TO GIVE MY BRAIN A POSITIVE KICK OF SOME KIND. IT'S LIKE THERE IS SOME CONNECTION BETWEEN LAUGHING AND REALLY TRULY FEELING BETTER ABOUT THINGS THAT WERE BOTHERING ME BEFORE. MAYBE LAUGHING JOSTLES SOME "HAPPINESS CONNECTORS" UP THERE. I LIKE TO WATCH POP'S STOMACH WHEN HE LAUGHS. IT SORT OF QUAKES. THE MORE I SEE THAT, THE MORE I LAUGH AND THE MORE I LAUGH THE MORE HE LAUGHS SO THE MORE QUAKES I HAVE TO LAUGH AT. SOME TIMES WE'LL MISS WHOLE SECTIONS OF RED SKELTON [A RADIO COMEDY SHOW] BECAUSE WE CAN'T STOP LAUGHING. I'M SO LUCKY TO BE A FRANKLIN. I LOVE YOU MOM AND YOU, TOO, "QUAKES". (SOMETIMES I JUST SLAY ME!!!)

AGE 8 [GRADE 6]
DI - I THINK I MADE A GREAT - IMPORTANT - DISCOVERY TODAY. I THINK THAT PEOPLE WHO DON'T HAVE A SENSE OF HUMOR ABOUT THEMSELVES ARE PEOPLE WHO FEEL

PRETTY BAD ABOUT THEMSELVES SO THEY TAKE THEIR LITTLE QUIRKS AND MISTAKES AS INDICATING A WEAKNESS THAT FURTHER PROVES HOW BAD OR INCOMPETENT THEY ARE. I HAVE BEEN WONDERING WHICH WAY IT WOULD HAVE TO WORK TO HELP THEM. MUST THEY LEARN TO LIKE THEMSELVES BETTER BEFORE THEY CAN LEARN TO ENJOY THEMSELVES AS THEY ARE OR COULD THEY BE TAUGHT TO LAUGH AT THEMSELVES TO HELP THEM START FEELING BETTER ABOUT THEMSELVES? POP SAYS MAYBE IT WORKS BOTH WAYS - THAT AS SUCH A PERSON SEES OTHERS ABLE TO ENJOY THEIR OWN FOIBLES, IT MAKES IT LEGITIMATE FOR THEM TO BEGIN SMILING AT THEIR OWN WITHOUT GETTING SO UPSET. IT'S LIKE MODELING THE CONCEPT THAT NO ONE HAS TO BE PERFECT AND THAT IN FACT IT IS OUR IMPERFECTIONS THAT PROVIDE MOST OF WHAT WE CALL HUMOR.

AGE 7 ½ [GRADE 5]
DEAR DI - I KNOW THAT BUDDY THINKS OF HIMSELF AS A GUY WITH A GREAT SENSE OF HUMOR BUT ALL HE EVER MAKES JOKES ABOUT IS OTHER PEOPLE'S PECULIARITIES OR DEFECTS (NEVER HIS OWN, BY THE WAY). I DON'T THINK THAT'S HUMOR. I THINK THAT'S JUST BEING HURTFUL AND MEAN. HE CAN'T TAKE THE SAME KIND OF KIDDING - I HAVE NOTICED THAT. GINNY SAYS SHE THINKS HE IS SAD ABOUT HIMSELF. HE HAS REASON TO WONDER ABOUT HIS OWN WORTH, I SUPPOSE. HE SURE NEVER GETS ANY BUILDING UP FROM HIS FAMILY. THEY SORT OF ALL JUST DO THE SAME TO EACH OTHER THAT BUDDY DOES TO THE OTHER KIDS. I DOUBT IF THAT'S HEREDITARY. MORE LIKELY LEARNED. MODELS ARE REALLY POWERFUL, AREN'T THEY. GINNY AND I HAVE DECIDED TO TAKE BUDDY ON AS A PROJECT AND SEE IF WE CAN'T GRADUALLY SHOW HIM WHAT IS REALLY GOOD AND IMPORTANT ABOUT BUDDY. WE THINK IT WILL BE GOOD PRACTICE FOR WHEN WE BECOME PARENTS.

POSITIVE, SOCIAL, AGREEMENT # 10

I WILL present myself with a humane sense of humor and learn to enjoy my own foibles

RATHER THAN spreading gloom, and being defensive about my personal weaknesses and mistakes and allowing them to lower my self-esteem,

BECAUSE people with a ready and active sense of humor tend to be healthier, happier, and more socially helpful people. Laughter and happiness produce chemicals within the body that contribute to our physical and mental health. When people become defensive, they then become fearful or angry, producing excess adrenaline and other chemicals, which not only tend to keep them fearful and angry but also contribute to poor physical health.

Topic Eleven:
The Positive Social Encounter

AGE 7 [GRADE FOUR]

DI - I HAVE SAID IT BEFORE - THE GROWN-UPS IN THIS TOWN LOVE THE STUFFING OUT OF ME. I'M GLAD THEY DO. THAT IS A GAUGE THAT I AM LIVING A PRETTY GOOD LIFE I THINK. (I WISH THE KIDS COULD LIKE ME THAT WELL.) I HAVE TRIED TO CONVINCE GINNY'S OLDER BROTHER, TOM, TO BE MORE LIKE ME. HE SAYS, "WHO CARES IF PEOPLE LIKE ME?" I THINK HE IS MISSING THE POINT. WE FRANKLINS ARE NOT NICE IN ORDER TO MAKE PEOPLE LIKE US. WE ARE NICE TO HELP OTHER PEOPLE FEEL BETTER. IT WOULD BE PRETTY SELFISH TO JUST DO STUFF TO MAKE YOURSELF POPULAR (ALTHOUGH BEING POPULAR WITH THE KIDS, FOR A CHANGE, WOULD REALLY BE NICE. SO MANY OF THEM SEEM TO HATE ME BECAUSE I'M SMART. (I KEEP TELLING GOD HE SHOULD TAKE SOME OF MY EXCESS INTELLIGENCE AND GIVE IT TO PETEY OR MR. DEETS - WE'D ALL BE BETTER OFF. I GOT SIDETRACKED.) WE (MOM, POP AND I) GET THE BIGGEST KICK OUT OF DOING THINGS FOR OTHER PEOPLE <u>ANONYMOUSLY</u> (THAT WORD LOOKS LIKE IT SHOULD MEAN 'THE UNKNOWN RODENT'). POP SAYS WHEN YOU TAKE CREDIT FOR YOUR CHARITY, IT'S LIKE WANTING TO PUT YOURSELF IN THE SPOTLIGHT RATHER THAN JUST WANTING TO BE HELPFUL. THAT'S VERY SELFISH I THINK. I AM NOT VERY GOOD AT KEEPING MOST SECRETS BUT I CAN ALWAYS KEEP 'CHARITY SECRETS' BECAUSE I FEEL SO MUCH MORE WONDERFUL INSIDE KNOWING I DID SOMETHING JUST FOR SOMEONE ELSE AND NOT FOR ME (ALTHOUGH I SUPPOSE DOING THINGS JUST TO GET THAT WONDERFUL FEELING WOULD BE SELFISH IN A WAY TOO. I WILL HAVE TO THINK ON THAT ONE.) IT ALL BOILS DOWN TO THIS, DI. I HAVE DECIDED THAT EVERY TIME I MEET SOMEONE ('ENCOUNTER' MIGHT BE A BETTER WORD THAN 'MEET') ENCOUNTER SOMEONE, I WILL TRY TO

BRING SOME JOY INTO THEIR LIFE. LIKE MY 'SMILIZING' CAMPAIGN WHEN I WAS A LITTLE KID [SEE, THE JOHNNY APPLESEED OF SMILES IN APPENDIX ONE] DID THAT SAME THING. I'M STILL LIKE "JOHNNY" I GUESS. I ALWAYS SMILE AND WAVE AND IF I'M CLOSE ENOUGH I CHAT (NOT ALWAYS A GOOD THING IN SCHOOL, OR DURING CHURCH, BUY THE WAY.) HAVE YOU NOTICED WHEN YOU ASK PEOPLE HOW THEY ARE, THEY ALMOST ALWAYS SAY FINE OR GOOD. (I ALWAYS SAY 'SUPER' WITH LOTS OF ENTHUSIASM, HOPING IT WILL RUB OFF). MY POINT WAS GOING TO BE THAT I THINK IT HELPS PEOPLE WHEN THEY HEAR THEMSELVES SAYING THEY FEEL FINE - LIKE IT HELPS THEM REALLY BELIEVE IT. MISS WOODS ALWAYS GOES INTO HER SONG AND DANCE ABOUT HER ACHES AND PAINS SO I DON'T ASK HER ANYMORE BECAUSE I THINK WHEN SHE HEARS HERSELF COMPLAINING SHE BELIEVE THAT AS WELL. I ALWAYS JUST TELL HER HOW GREAT SHE LOOKS (THAT WAS MOM'S SOLUTION TO THE PROBLEM, REALLY.) "IT'S SURE NICE TO SEE YOU LOOKING SO FIT TODAY, MISS WOODS." I EVEN USUALLY GET A SMILE FROM HER, NOW. THANKS FOR LISTENING DI. YOU'RE LOOKING PRETTY GOOD TONIGHT, YOURSELF. HA! HA!

POSITIVE, SOCIAL, AGREEMENT # 11

I WILL sincerely try to leave each person I encounter in a more positive condition than he was when I encountered him,

RATHER THAN ignore or merely put down, degrade or antagonize him,

BECAUSE people who are treated in positive, supportive ways both feel better about themselves and the world they line in, and tend to engage in (pass on) positive encounters to others. [See Johnny Appleseed article in *Appendix One*.]

Topic Twelve:
The importance of modeling one's values

AGE 6 [GRADE 2]
DEAR DIARY,
POP SAYS IF YOU BELIEVE SOMETHING IS RIGHT, YOU SHOULD LET PEOPLE KNOW IT AND THAT THE BEST WAY TO DO THAT IS TO <u>SHOW</u> PEOPLE THROUGH HOW YOU LIVE. MOM AND POP BELIEVE IN BEING FRIENDLY, HELPFUL PEOPLE. I GUESS I JUST CAUGHT THE FRIENDLY AND THE HELPFUL FROM THEM BECAUSE I SEE I AM THAT WAY, TOO. IT IS HARD TO UNDERSTAND HOW SOMEBODY COULD NOT SHOW WHAT THEY BELIEVE IN. IF YOU BELIEVE IN BEING POLITE YOU WOULD NOT GO AROUND BEING RUDE. I THINK IT IS HARDER TO SHOW WHAT YOU DO <u>NOT</u> BELIEVE IN - I MEAN WHAT YOU ARE AGAINST. I AM PERSONALLY VERY MUCH AGAINST WAR BUT I AM NOT SURE HOW I CAN SHOW THAT EVERY DAY. I MEAN PEOPLE SEE THAT I DON'T GO OUT AND START WARS BUT LITTLE KIDS DON'T GO AND START WARS. I DO NOT FIGHT, SO MAYBE THAT IS THE LITTLE KID'S VERSION OF NOT STARTING WARS. MOM SAYS ABIDING BY THE RULES IS ONE WAY TO BE A GOOD MODEL. I AM SURE SHE IS RIGHT BUT WHAT ABOUT DUMB RULES? I CAN SEE THAT I AM GOING TO HAVE A PROBLEM WITH DUMB RULES. MISS DISTLEMIER IS GENERALLY A GREAT TEACHER AND NICE HUMAN BEING. BUT SHE HAS TWO RULES I THINK ARE REALLY DUMB. ONE IS, "NO SQUIRMING IN YOUR SEAT." I TOLD HER I WAS SORRY BUT I BELIEVE I WAS BORN SQUIRMING BECAUSE I CANNOT REMEMBER A INSTANCE LONGER THAN A FEW MINUTES WHEN I WASN'T SQUIRMING. IT IS LIKE THERE IS A PART OF MY BRAIN THAT IS ON A TIMER AND EVERY FEW MINUTES IT SENDS OUT A MESSAGE TO MY LOWER QUARTERS THAT SAYS, "GO, BUTT! GO!" IN ORDER NOT TO SQUIRM, I WOULD HAVE TO DO NOTHING BUT THINK ABOUT NOT SQUIRMING AND IT IS MY OPINION THAT AFTER SEVERAL HOURS MY

BRAIN WOULD JUST EXPLODE FROM ALL THAT EFFORT. THE GOOD THING ABOUT THAT WOULD BE IT WOULD MAKE ALL OF THE GIRLS SCREAM AND PROBABLY EVEN RUN OUT INTO THE HALL - THAT WOULD BE GREAT! WHAT I AM GETTING TO IS THAT I AM NEVER GOING TO BE A GOOD MODEL OF THE "DON'T SQUIRM" RULE AND JUST HOW THAT CAUSES A PROBLEM FOR MY LEARNING I CAN NOT FIGURE OUT - I DO NOT LEARN WITH <u>THAT</u> PART OF MY ANATOMY. (<u>THAT</u> IS PRETTY FUNNY!!!) THE OTHER DUMB RULE IS "NO WHISTLING WHILE YOU WORK." I WILL NOT GO IN TO THAT ONE HERE BUT I SUSPECT SHE MADE THAT RULE JUST FOR ME. POP SAYS ONCE I LEARNED TO WHISTLE I NEVER STOPPED. . . . GOT TO GO TO SLEEP NOW. IT STARTED SNOWING AT SUNSET SO BY FOUR A.M. I NEED TO BE OUT THERE SHOVELING WALKS FOR THE OLD FOLKS. THAT WILL BE GREAT! I'LL START AT MRS. STEPHENS AND THEN GO TO MR. DEETS.

POSITIVE, SOCIAL, AGREEMENT # 12

I WILL consistently model these agreements to others in all aspects of my daily life,

RATHER THAN giving lip service to them and behaving in ways contrary to these agreements,

BECAUSE a positive value can only make a positive impact if it is regularly modeled, and modeling contradictory values can only be hurtful to society and man's circumstances.

Topic Thirteen:
Honesty, Tact, and Integrity

AGE 6 [GRADE TWO]
DEAR DIARY,
    I FIND IT HARD TO KNOW HOW TO BE HONEST AND TACTFUL AT THE SAME TIME. WHEN MRS. HARNER ASKED ME AFTER SUNDAY SCHOOL THIS MORNING IF I ENJOYED HER LESSON, I DIDN'T KNOW WHAT TO SAY. IT WAS - IN ALL HONESTY - THE DUMBEST LESSON I'VE EVER HAD TO SIT THROUGH. IT WAS FILLED WITH MISINFORMATION AND UNFOUNDED OPINION. SO, IN ALL HONESTY, I COULD HAVE SAID, I DIDN'T LIKE IT AT ALL. BUT SINCE MOM, POP AND PARSON HAVE LAUNCHED THIS CAMPAIGN TO REBUILD CRAIGY AS A TACTFUL YOUNG MAN, I DECIDED I SHOULDN'T DO THAT. SO, I HAD SOME OPTIONS. I COULD SAY, "IT SURE GAVE ME THINGS TO THINK ABOUT," WHICH IT DID - ABOUT HOW SUNDAY SCHOOL TEACHERS CAN BE SO DUMB AND STILL BE ALLOWED TO TEACH - NO , TO MISINFORM - THE KIDS. I COULD HAVE SAID, "I THINK IT WAS AMONG YOUR BEST LESSONS," WHICH IT WAS - THEY ARE ALL TERRIBLE. WHAT I SAID INSTEAD WAS, "I REALLY ENJOYED COLORING JOSEPH'S COAT OF MANY COLORS." I PROBABLY SHOULD HAVE LEFT OUT THE 'REALLY' BUT HEY, I'M NEW AT THIS. I UNDERSTAND IT IS IMPORTANT NOT TO PUT PEOPLE DOWN AND TO BUILD THEM UP FOR THEIR STRONG POINTS. I JUST HAVE TO WONDER IF AVOIDING THE 'REAL' TRUTH BY SIDESTEPPING IT, ISN'T ONE OF THOSE SINS OF OMISSION THAT PARSON TENDS TO PREACH ABOUT (ALL TOO OFTEN!). I HAVE DECIDED NOT TO DEFINE TACT-BASED OMISSIONS AS SINS BECAUSE WHAT I AM TRYING TO DO IS TO BE HELPFUL TO THE PERSON IN A DIFFERENT REALM FROM THE HONEST-DISHONEST REALM. I AM WORKING IN THE REALM OF SELF-ESTEEM INSTEAD. I WON'T LIE AND SAY SOMETHING IS GREAT WHEN IT IS

TERRIBLE AND I WON'T SAY I REALLY LIKE SOMETHING IF I DON'T (I CAN SAY, "I SURE APPRECIATE YOUR THOUGHTFULNESS.") HOWEVER I DO IT, I STILL HAVE TO MAKE IT FIT MY BELIEFS ABOUT BEING A NICE, HELPFUL, PERSON. LIVING A GOOD LIFE TAKES A LOT MORE PLANNING AND EFFORT THAN I THOUGHT IT WOULD - BUT THEN, I STILL BELIEVE NOTHING IS MORE IMPORTANT THAN DOING THAT. DI, I WORE MYSELF OUT JUST THINKING ABOUT IT. NIGHT, NIGHT.

AGE 9 ½ [GRADE 8]
DEAR DI. - DECISIONS BETWEEN RIGHT AND WRONG ARE OFTEN DIFFICULT FOR ME. SOMETIMES IT SEEMS WHAT IS RIGHT FOR ME IS NOT RIGHT FOR OTHERS AND VISA VERSA. LIKE TODAY IN P. E. - IT WAS GOING TO BE TOUCH FOOTBALL - COACH SAID SO YESTERDAY. IN MY CLASS THE TERM 'TOUCH' MEANS, "TOUCH CRAIGY HARD ENOUGH THAT HE ENDS UP FLAT ON HIS FACE - OVER AND OVER AND OVER AGAIN." THEY HATE ME. I TRY TO BE NICE TO THEM BUT I'M ALWAYS JUST THE PESKY LITTLE TWIRP THAT RUINS THE GRADE CURVE. I CAN EVEN UNDERSTAND THAT. ANYWAY, I WENT TO SCHOOL EARLY AND WROTE PRINCIPAL MARTIN A NOTE THAT I HAD BORROWED HIS PHYSICS BOOK AND WAS GOING TO THE CREEK FOR THE DAY BECAUSE I WAS AFRAID TO GO TO P. E. I THOUGHT HE SHOULD KNOW WHERE I WAS IN CASE THERE WAS AN EMERGENCY. I WONDERED IF HE WOULD COME AND DRAG ME BACK TO SCHOOL - LIKE HE HAS DONE ON OTHER OCCASIONS THOUGH NOT FOR A LONG TIME, COME TO THINK OF IT. I KNOW IT WAS WRONG TO SKIP SCHOOL AND THAT MOM AND POP WOULD BE DISAPPOINTED ABOUT IT BUT I ALSO KNOW IT IS WRONG FOR THOSE BIG FRESH<u>MEAN</u> (AN INTERESTING FREUDIAN SLIP) FRESH<u>MAN</u> BOYS TO HURT ME FOR THE SHEER FUN OF IT. TO HAVE A SENSE OF INTEGRITY A PERSON HAS TO DO, EVERY DAY, WHAT HE BELIEVES IS RIGHT. TONIGHT I DON'T FEEL THAT SENSE OF INTEGRITY DEEP DOWN

INSIDE ME, BUT YOU KNOW WHAT, DI? I DON'T THINK I'D FEEL IT IF I HAD GONE TO SCHOOL EITHER. THINGS ARE NO LONGER BLACK AND WHITE. BUT THEN, TONIGHT, AT LEAST, I'M NOT BLACK AND BLUE AND THAT MUST COUNT FOR SOMETHING.

AGE 9 ½ [GRADE 9]
    DI - I HAD A TALK WITH DOC TODAY ABOUT INTEGRITY. I REALLY HAD A QUESTION BUT SOMETIMES WITH DOC ASKING A QUESTION GETS YOU NOWHERE FAST BECAUSE HE TOSSES IT RIGHT BACK ON ME SO I JUST TALKED AROUND THE TOPIC FOR A WHILE. MY PROBLEM IS THAT I AM COMING TO SEE THAT BEING A PERSON OF INTEGRITY DOES NOT NECESSARILY MEAN THAT PERSON'S BELIEFS ARE ONES I CAN RESPECT. AS I UNDERSTAND IT, INTEGRITY REFERS TO LIVING UP TO ONE'S POSITIVE BELIEFS AND STANDING BY THEM REGARDLESS. BOTH DOC AND PARSON ARE SUCH MEN. THEY ARE BOTH GOOD MEN BUT THE BELIEFS THEY EACH HOLD [TO HAVE INTEGRITY ABOUT] ARE RATHER DIFFERENT. I RESPECT THEM BOTH FOR HAVING INTEGRITY. BUT I CAN NOT HOLD THE BELIEFS OF ONE IF I HOLD THE BELIEFS OF THE OTHER. PARSON IS A GOOD MAN BECAUSE HE BELIEVES GOD SAYS HE HAS TO BE - OR ELSE! DOC IS A GOOD MAN BECAUSE IT JUST MAKES SENSE TO HIM TO BE THAT WAY FOR THE GOOD OF PEOPLE IN GENERAL. THE TWO MEN RESPECT EACH OTHER FROM A DISTANCE THOUGH THEY BOTH BELIEVE THE OTHER IS MISGUIDED IN TERMS OF MOTIVATION. I GUESS THEY SHARE AN END PURPOSE - THE BETTERMENT OF THE HUMAN CONDITION - BUT THEY ARE COMING AT IT FROM DIFFERENT MOTIVATIONS. I WONDER IF MAYBE JUST BEING GOOD AND HELPFUL IS NOT MORE IMPORTANT THAN WHY ONE IS BEING GOOD AND HELPFUL. THERE SEEM TO BE SO MANY MORE BIG QUESTIONS AS I GET OLDER.

POSITIVE, SOCIAL, AGREEMENT # 13

I WILL approach my self and my fellow men with honesty presented with tact and integrity,

RATHER THAN being deceitful or deceptive or abruptly honest in a hurtful manner,

BECAUSE honesty builds close, helpful, comfortable relationships and trust, while dishonesty fosters mistrust, discomfort and division.

Topic Fourteen:
Maintaining one's focus on the inappropriate *behavior*

AGE 7 ½ [GRADE 5]
DEAR DI - I SPENT THE DAY IN PRINCIPAL MARTIN'S OFFICE. MY TEACHER AND I HAD A DISAGREEMENT OVER BUTCHIE'S BASIC VALUE AS A HUMAN BEING. SHE CALLED HIM A BAD BOY AND I POINTED OUT TO HER THAT HE WAS ACTUALLY A PRETTY GOOD HUMAN BOY - TALL, STRONG, HEALTHY, GOOD VISION AND HEARING, AND NOT UNINTELLIGENT. I WAS TRYING TO POINT OUT TO HER THAT IT WASN'T 'HIM' THAT WAS BAD. IT WAS THE WAY HE ACTED SOMETIMES - WELL USUALLY - THAT WAS 'BAD' AND THAT I DIDN'T THINK IT WAS THE CHRISTIAN THING TO DO TO CONFUSE THE TWO. ONCE I SAW THAT HER CHEEK WAS TWITCHING I REALIZED I WASN'T LONG FOR THE ROOM SO I FORGED AHEAD TO GIVE HER ONE MORE THING TO THINK ABOUT. "WHEN BUTCHIE IS AT MY HOME HIS BEHAVIOR IS EXCELLENT AND MY PARENTS THINK HE'S A PLEASANT LAD - THEY HAVE SAID SO. PERHAPS YOU SHOULD CONSIDER WHAT THERE IS ABOUT YOUR CLASSROOM THAT LEADS HIM TO MISBEHAVE HERE. (I'LL BE IN THE OFFICE FOR THE REST OF THE WEEK, BY THE WAY. IT IS ALWAYS A RELIEF TO KNOW I WON'T HAVE TO BE IN HER ROOM FOR A WHILE.) EVENTUALLY I WILL HAVE TO APOLOGIZE TO HER. I WILL APOLOGIZE FOR TALKING ABOUT THAT IN FRONT OF THE OTHER CHILDREN - THAT WAS PROBABLY POOR JUDGMENT - BUT NOT ABOUT THE IDEAS I EXPRESSED - AND MR. MARTIN KNOWS THAT BY NOW. I KNOW MAKING THAT DISTINCTION BETWEEN THE PERSON AND THE BEHAVIOR IS NOT MY ORIGINAL IDEA BUT I BELIEVE IT. I THINK IT GIVES MORE HOPE FOR CHANGE. IF A PERSON WERE BAD JUST BECAUSE HE WAS BUILT THAT WAY THERE WOULDN'T BE MUCH CHANCE OF HELPING HIM CHANGE, BUT IF IT'S ONLY THE WAY HE HAS LEARNED TO ACT YOU HAVE A GOOD CHANCE TO DO SOMETHING HELPFUL FOR HIM. I

THINK JUST THAT ONE CHANGE IN MOST TEACHER'S PERSPECTIVES, AND CLASSROOMS WOULD BECOME HAPPIER AND HEALTHIER PLACES FOR KIDS. (I LIKE THAT, DI. HAPPY, HEALTHY CLASSROOMS - OR SHOULD THAT BE HEALTHFUL?) LOTS OF TIMES, IT SEEMS, A CLASSROOM IS SET UP MORE TO MEET THE TEACHER'S NEEDS THAN THE KID'S. PRETTY BACKWARDS, I'D SAY. BACK TO MY BEHAVIOR FOR A MINUTE. I'M A REALLY NICE KID - I'M HELPFUL AND COMPASSIONATE AND I GO OUT OF MY WAY TO POINT OUT CHANGES TEACHERS CAN MAKE TO DO A BETTER JOB. (I STILL HAVE SOME DIFFICULTY UNDERSTANDING WHY MY GOOD INTENTIONS KEEP GETTING ME INTO TROUBLE) THAT'S INTERESTING. I SELDOM EVER REALLY GET INTO TROUBLE. I GET SENT TO THE OFFICE BUT I'VE NEVER GOTTEN A SPANKING - I'VE NEVER BEEN STOOD IN THE CORNER - I'VE NEVER BEEN SENT HOME. I TELL MR. MARTIN WHAT HAPPENED AND HE SIGHS (THAT'S HIS ONLY OUTWARD REACTION, USUALLY). THEN HE ASKS IF I UNDERSTAND WHY MY TEACHER GOT UPSET. THAT GIVES ME A CHANCE TO SPEND A FEW MINUTES OUTLINING HER SPECIFIC MENTAL HEALTH PROBLEMS. WHEN I STOP TALKING, HE NODS ME TOWARD THE TABLE WHERE I SETTLE IN FOR THE DAY. IT IS A GOOD ARRANGEMENT I THINK. I LOVE THAT CORNER IN HIS OFFICE. IT'S QUIET AND I CAN READ AND WRITE. HE USUALLY DOESN'T EVEN MIND IF I HUM OR WHISTLE. FOR SOME REASON, THAT DRIVES TEACHERS WILD. THEY SAY I'M A BAD BOY FOR DOING IT. THEY SAY I'M DISTURBING THE OTHER KIDS. I'VE NEVER HAD THEM COMPLAIN. IF YOU ASK ME, IT'S THE SUPER QUIET CLASSROOM THAT IS UNNATURAL AND UNNERVING TO MOST KIDS. NORMAL KIDS NEVER WANT THINGS TO BE QUIET. I GUESS TEACHERS FORGET HOW IT WAS. I DO WISH THAT WHEN I DID SOMETHING THAT BUGGED THEM THEY WOULDN'T THINK OF ME AS A THROUGH AND THROUGH BAD PERSON. THAT JUST MAKES NO SENSE. THAT REALLY IS NOT FAIR BECAUSE IT SEEMS TO THROW OUT <u>ALL</u> THE

GOOD IN ME BASED ON THAT ONE DEED. PEOPLE THINK STRANGE OR IS THAT STRANGELY. I GOT IT, STRANGE PEOPLE THINK STRANGELY.

POSITIVE, SOCIAL, AGREEMENT # 14

I WILL react to inappropriate behaviors, goals, and ideas for what they are

RATHER THAN reacting negatively to the person who holds them
,
BECAUSE I can disapprove of what a person does or proposes without disapproving of him or her. I will refrain from thoughts such as, "I hate *him* for what he did," thinking instead, "I dislike (or even hate, perhaps) *what he did*." Once a person becomes the object of hate, traits such as compassion, love, and helpfulness come to a halt. If, on the other hand, you have separated the disliked or unacceptable act or idea from the still love-worthy person, he or she is not the object of hate and your basic, positive, humanity centered nature can be utilized to evaluate and help solve the dilemma.

Topic Fifteen:

The necessary effort to understand each other's meaning

AGE 9 ½ [GRADE NINE]

DI - I DON'T KNOW IF YOU'VE NOTICED, DI, BUT THE EXACT SAME WORD CAN MEAN VERY DIFFERENT THINGS TO DIFFERENT PEOPLE. LIKE WHEN MR. STOUT ASKS ME HOW MUCH I'LL CHARGE HIM TO SHOVEL HIS WALK AND I SAY TEN CENTS AND HE SAYS "THAT'S ACCEPTABLE", HE MEANS IT'S A GOOD AND FAIR PRICE AND WE HAVE A DEAL. WHEN MISS BAHR HANDS BACK PAPERS TO KIDS WHO GET C'S SHE SAYS "THAT'S ACCEPTABLE" BUT SHE MEANS IT'S REALLY JUST ONE STEP AWAY FROM BEING REALLY BAD ('POOR' WOULD BE A BETTER WORD). PASTOR SAYS OLD MISS ELZER IS A BEAUTIFUL PERSON. I HAVE TO ASSUME HE'S SPEAKING ABOUT THE FACT THAT SHE'S A REALLY NICE PERSON BECAUSE SHE IS THE GOSH UGLIEST LADY (NO OFFENCE, GOD! YOU DID YOUR BEST, I'M SURE.) THAT I'VE EVER SEEN. PEOPLE SAY BABIES ARE BEAUTIFUL BUT I'LL TELL YOU I'VE SEEN A LOT OF THEM AND I'VE NEVER SEEN ONE THAT RATED ANYTHING ABOVE MILDLY UGLY - MARY PERRY'S NEW BABY LOOKS LIKE WINSTON CHURCHILL WITH BLOTCHES AND THAT'S NOT BEAUTIFUL. PEOPLE MUST MEAN THE IDEA OF A NEW LITTLE HUMAN BEING IS A BEAUTIFUL EVENT. THEN THERE'S "BEHAVIOR YOURSELF" - PROBABLY THE WORST DIRECTIVE EVER INVENTED. MOM AND POP SELDOM USE THAT TERM, THOUGH IF THEY DO I HAVE A CLEAR UNDERSTANDING OF WHAT IT MEANS - "LIVE UP TO OUR FAMILY PURPOSE". WHEN MISS ACHER SAID IT IN THIRD GRADE, SHE MEANT "SHUT UP, SIT DOWN, AND STAY THAT WAY 'TIL MY MIGRAINE GOES AWAY. (SHE HAD A LOT OF MIGRAINES THE SEMESTER I WAS IN HER ROOM SO I DON'T THINK I GOT HER BEST TEACHING.) WHEN MISS DISTLEMEIR SAID

IT, SHE MEANT, "BE A NICE PERSON." I WAS NEVER QUITE ENTIRELY SURE WHAT MR. JACKS MEANT - THE COUNSELOR AT CHURCH CAMP. WHEN I ASKED HIM TO DEFINE THAT TERM FOR US THE VEIN IN HIS FOREHEAD BEGAN THROBBING AND HE SENT ME BACK TO THE CABIN. I HAVE TO ASSUME THAT HE DID NOT CONSIDER ASKING FOR CLARIFICATION AS 'BEHAVING'. THE WHOLE CHURCH CAMP THING WAS STRANGE THAT WAY. I'D ASK QUESTIONS AND REQUEST CLARIFICATION AND VERIFICATION OF THINGS THE LEADERS WERE TELLING US ABOUT GOD AND RELIGION AND THEY'D TELL ME TO JUST STOP ROCKING THE BOAT. IT WAS REALLY A RELIEF WHEN I LEARNED THE CAMP STAFF HAD REQUESTED THAT I NOT RETURN NEXT YEAR. I ONLY HEARD A LITTLE BIT OF THE CONVERSATION BETWEEN POP AND PARSON, BUT WHAT I HEARD WAS SOMETHING LIKE POP SAYING, "IF YOUR TEACHINGS ARE SO SHALLOW THEY CAN'T WITHSTAND THE SCRUTINY OF A NINE YEAR OLD, I CAN SEE NO BENEFIT FROM MY SON CONTINUING TO ATTEND YOUR CAMP." (GO POP!!!) THERE ARE LOTS MORE EXAMPLES, DI, BUT WHAT THEY TELL ME IS THAT I MUST NEVER ASSUME SOMEBODY ELSE MEANS THE EXACT SAME THING THAT I WOULD MEAN WHEN I USED THAT WORD. IT PUTS A BIG RESPONSIBILITY ON THE ONE WHO IS LISTENING. MAYBE THAT'S WHY SO FEW FOLKS EVER SEEM TO TALK FOR LONG ABOUT SUBJECTS OF SUBSTANCE. DOWN AT THE FEED STORE [THE GATHERING PLACE FOR COFFEE AND CHECKERS FOR THE OLDER MEN IN THE COMMUNITY] IT COULD MATTER LESS WHAT WORDS REALLY MEAN BECAUSE NOBODY DOES MUCH MORE THAN BRAG ABOUT THEMSELVES AND PUT DOWN THE GUYS WHO AREN'T THERE. WHILE ONE GUY BRAGS, THE OTHERS SEEM MORE INTENT ON THINKING UP SOME STORY TO TOP WHAT'S BEING SAID THAN ON LISTENING. I HAVE DETERMINED THROUGH CAREFUL STUDY THAT TEN MEN AT THE FEED STORE CAN TALK TO (NOT WITH) EACH OTHER FOR UP TO A FULL HOUR WITHOUT EVER REALLY SAYING ANYTHING

MEANINGFUL. THERE IS AS BIG DIFFERENCE BETWEEN TALKING AND COMMUNICATING - DOC SAID THAT AND I CAN SEE IT IS TRUE. WHAT I DON'T UNDERSTAND IS WHY THE GUYS AT THE FEED STORE SEEM TO ENJOY IT ALL SO MUCH. MAYBE IT'S JUST BEING CLOSE WITH YOUR FRIENDS - THAT'S WHAT POP THINKS. WHATEVER IT IS, IT CERTAINLY IS NOT BECOMING ENLIGHTENED ABOUT ANYTHING NEW.

AGE 7 [GRADE 5]
DEAR DIARY,
       I GOT INTO HOT WATER AGAIN TODAY, DI. I TOLD MY TEACHER IT APPEARED TO ME THAT HOW SHE WAS TRYING TO TEACH THE SLOWER KIDS TO MULTIPLY FRACTIONS WAS INAPPROPRIATE AND THAT I HAD A SUGGESTION FOR HER. I SAID IT ALL IN PRIVATE AND NOBODY ELSE HEARD A THING. SHE SENT ME TO THE OFFICE WITH A NOTE EXPLAINING THAT I HAD CALLED HER A _BAD_ TEACHER AND THAT SHE WOULD NOT STAND FOR THAT. (_STAND FOR_ - THAT IS FUNNY, DI, BECAUSE SHE COMES IN, IN THE MORNING, AND _SITS_ BEHIND HER DESK AND DOESN'T LEAVE THERE ALL DAY.) ANYWAY I EXPLAINED TO MR. MARTIN THAT I HAD USED THE WORD _INAPPROPRIATE_ AND THAT I HAD INTENDED NOTHING THAT MEANT THERE WAS ANYTHING _BAD_ ABOUT HER - JUST THAT HER METHOD CLEARLY WAS NOT WORKING AND I HAD A SUGGESTION FOR HER. IF SHE HAD LET ME CONTINUE I COULD HAVE TOLD HER THAT I HAD TRIED MY WAY WITH JUNIOR (NO OTHER NAME, JUST JUNIOR) AND IT HAD WORKED WELL. I GOT THE USUAL LECTURE ABOUT JUST NOT ROCKING THE BOAT BECAUSE I KNEW HOW SENSITIVE THAT TEACHER WAS. WELL, DI, I'LL TELL YOU ONE THING - TWO THINGS. I DON'T THINK IT IS RIGHT FOR HER TO SAY I CALLER HER A _BAD_ TEACHER WHEN I DIDN'T AND I DON'T THINK IT IS FAIR TO THE SLOW KIDS FOR HER TO IGNORE MY METHOD WHICH I HAVE ALREADY PROVED IS BETTER THAN HERS. I GUESS

I'LL JUST HAVE TO GET THEM TOGETHER AFTER SCHOOL. THEN TOMORROW ON THE TEST THEY WILL DO OKAY AND SHE WILL LOOK AT ME SAY, "SEE, I'M NOT SUCH A BAD TEACHER AFTER ALL," AND ACCORDING TO MR. MARTIN I'M JUST SUPPOSED TO SIT THERE AND SAY NOTHING. IF I WERE REALLY INTO <u>FAIR AND UNFAIR</u> THIS ONE WOULD <u>BLOW MY GASKETS</u>. GRRRRRRRRRRRRRRR!!!!!!!!

POSITIVE, SOCIAL, AGREEMENT # 15

I WILL make certain that I understand what another person means (intends) by the words he or she uses before I react to them,

RATHER THAN assuming, others mean the same things that I mean when using the same words,

BECAUSE the sole purpose of words is to communicate the *speaker's* meaning and intentions, so it is only the speaker's meaning, not the listener's meaning, that counts. We, therefore, never respond with, "But that's not what <u>you</u> said," but rather, "<u>I</u> didn't understand what you meant."

Topic Sixteen:
Use of specific terms

AGE 8 [GRADE SIX]
DEAR DI,
     HERE'S A NEW ONE FOR YOU. "SWEARING IS THE HALLMARK OF A LAZY MIND." HOW ABOUT THAT? I'VE BEEN STUDYING THE PEOPLE WHO SWEAR A LOT. IF THEY WOULD JUST TAKE THE TIME TO USE THE WORD THEY REALLY MEAN, THEN EVERYONE WOULD KNOW EXACTLY WHAT THEY MEAN. AS LONG AS THEY JUST SWEAR, I'LL NEVER KNOW. I ALSO GET THE IDEA THE SWEARER REALLY DOESN'T KNOW EITHER, SO THAT MUST REALLY CONFUSE HIS MIND AND HIS FEELINGS. LIKE WHEN BUTCHIE SAID, "I HATE THE GD (SORRY, BUT THAT IS WHAT HE SAID - WELL, IT IS THE INITIALS OF WHAT HE SAID!) TEACHERS BECAUSE THEY TREAT ME LIKE XXXX." I DOUBT IF HE REALLY STOPPED TO SPECIFY IN HIS MIND WHAT HE REALLY MEANT BY GD - 'UNFAIR' MAYBE, 'HURTFUL', 'BELLIGERENT', 'PREJUDICED'? YOU SEE, IF HE KNEW AND USED THE RIGHT WORD THEN HE AND I WOULD BOTH HAVE SOMEWHERE TO START TO SOLVE HIS PROBLEMS ABOUT THE TEACHERS. AND HOW DOES HE SAY THEY TREAT HIM (XXXX)? WHO KNOWS - 'UNFAIRLY', 'LIKE HE'S WORTHLESS', 'LIKE HE'S DUMB'? MY POINT IS THAT SWEARING ALWAYS SEEMS TO BE QUITE NON-SPECIFIC AND UNREVEALING OF ANYTHING HELPFUL EXCEPT PERHAPS EMOTION. THERE ARE A LOT OF OTHER NON-SPECIFIC WORDS PEOPLE USE IN A SIMILAR WAY - IT'S LIKE THEY (THE WORDS) KEEP THEM FROM HAVING TO THINK ABOUT OR SPECIFY WHAT THEY REALLY MEAN (SO WHY EVEN TALK ABOUT IT, THEN?) 'THING' IS SUCH A WORD. 'THEY', LIKE WHEN PEOPLE SAY, "THEY SAY THAT BLA BLA BLA IS TRUE." I'VE DECIDED THAT 'THEY' IS ALWAYS AN UNRELIABLE SOURCE PROVIDING QUESTIONABLE INFORMATION THAT SELDOM HAS BASIS IN SCIENTIFIC FACT OR LOGICAL CONCLUSIONS.

'SOMETHING' IS ANOTHER ONE - "LET'S GO DO SOMETHING, OKAY?" HOW CAN I ANSWER UNTIL THE SPEAKER HAS CLARIFIED WHAT 'SOMETHING' WILL BE?

ANYWAY, WHAT THIS IS ALL LEADING UP TO IS TO REMIND MYSELF TO STOP USING NON-SPECIFICS (I DON'T CUSS, DI, REALLY) AND TO TRY AND HELP THOSE WHO DO TO AT LEAST BE AWARE OF IT IF NOT ALSO TRY AND SPEAK MORE MEANINGFULLY. . . .

MY CUBBIES LOST AGAIN - BIG SURPRISE! IT CERTAINLY TRIES ONE'S PATIENCE TO BE A CUBS FAN. IT'S STRANGE HOW I CAN BE PATIENT ABOUT THAT BUT IT DRIVES ME NUTS WAITING IN LINE FOR A DRINK AFTER RECESS. POP ALWAYS CLAIMS TO BE A SOX FAN BUT I NOTICE HE ALWAYS HANGS AROUND TO LISTEN TO THE CUBS GAMES. RADIO IS REALLY GREAT, YOU KNOW, DI. (WOOPS! BY 'GREAT' I MEANT A WONDERFUL MODERN COMMUNICATIONS CONVENIENCE.) HA! HA! GO CUBBIES!!!!

POSITIVE, SOCIAL, AGREEMENT # 16

I WILL, when communicating, use specific, precise, terms

RATHER THAN using non-specific, generalizations ("Everybody does it."), or lazy speech ("thing", "they say", "you know", and the laziest of all, profanity,

BECAUSE non-specific words and phrases carry little or no content meaning (though they often suggest emotions which can be more appropriately be expressed with a precise term) and allow imprecise thinking and thereby wrong conclusions.

Topic Seventeen:
The careful and judicious use of categories and *category words*

AGE 8 ½ [GRADE 7]

DI - <u>CATEGORIES</u> ARE FUNNY THINGS - WELL, NOT FUNNY HA, HA, BUT FUNNY STRANGE. THEY ARE TROUBLESOMELY (I WONDER IF THAT'S A WORD) DECEPTIVE. I THINK IT'S BECAUSE CATEGORIES MAKE OUR LIVES SO EASY THAT WE BEGIN DEPENDING ON THEM FOR THINGS THEY ARE NEVER INTENDED TO IMPLY OR INCLUDE. LIKE THE CHEERLEADER CATEGORY. WE ALL KNOW WHO FITS INTO THAT CATEGORY. IT'S NOT THE REFEREES OR THE MASCOT. IT'S NOT THE PEOPLE IN THE STANDS OR THE TEAM MEMBERS. IT'S A HELPFUL CATEGORY WORD - YOU SEE, DI. IT REFERS TO THE GIRLS WHO DRESS UP IN STRANGE, DRAFTY COSTUMES AND YELL OUT INANE SAYINGS IN A MONOTONOUS, REPETITIVE, FASHION WHICH, FOR SOME REASON, FANS THE FANS INTO HYSTERIA. (I SUSPECT IT MAY BE THE SHORT SKIRTS AND THE JUMPING UP AND DOWN - IT CERTAINLY COULD NOT BE WHAT THEY ACTUALLY SAY.) MOST OF THEM ARE PRETTY GIRLS WITH EXCEPTIONALLY LARGE CHESTS WHO APPARENTLY DON'T EAT ENOUGH (AT LEAST THEY STAY MORE SLENDER FROM THE CHEST DOWN THAN SEEMS REASONABLE.) ONE TEAM WHO VISITED US HAD A BOY CHEERLEADER. HE WAS VERY PRETTY, ALSO, I THOUGHT. SO, IT'S A USEFUL CATEGORY WHEN IT'S ONLY USED LIKE IT'S INTENDED. BUT THE PROBLEM COMES INTO A CATEGORY WHEN YOU START ADDING IN TRAITS THAT AREN'T REALLY IMPLIED BY THE TERM. LIKE ALL CHEERLEADERS ARE SNOOTY OR VAIN OR DUMB OR BOY CRAZY (OR TOO THIN, SHAME ON ME). IT'S LIKE SAYING ALL CHINAMEN ARE SNEAKY OR ALL GYPSIES ARE THIEVES OR ALL NEGROES ARE LAZY OR ALL WOMEN ARE WEAK OR ALL WHITE FOLKS ARE PREJUDICED. A CHINAMAN IS FROM CHINESE ANCESTRY - PERIOD. NEGROES BELONG TO

A CERTAIN GENE POOL AND ARE GENERALLY BLACK - PERIOD. WOMEN ARE ADULT FEMALES, PERIOD. AND SO ON. IT IS LIKE GENIUSES - WE ARE ALL SMART - PERIOD. WE DON'T ALL WEAR GLASSES AND CARRY BOOKS EVERYWHERE AND SHUN SPORTS PARTICIPATION. SMART! PERIOD! BUT EVEN TEACHERS SEEM TO ADD UNINTENDED TRAITS TO THE CATEGORY LIKE MORE MATURE, WISER, MORE DEPENDABLE. THOSE THINGS AREN'T IMPLIED BY THE WORD GENIUS. THE KIDS THINK I'M WEAK AND THAT I THINK I'M BETTER THAN OTHER PEOPLE. THEY THINK I'M A SHOW-OFF BECAUSE I GET ALL A'S. IT'S A CATEGORY PROBLEM YOU SEE, DI. I THINK IT'S ONE OF THE MOST VIRULENT (I THINK THAT MEANS REALLY, REALLY DESTRUCTIVE) SOCIAL PROBLEMS. PEOPLE NATURALLY DEPEND ON CATEGORIES TO MAKE COMMUNICATION EASIER AND MAYBE BECAUSE THEY (CATEGORIES) ARE SO DEPENDABLE AND WE JUST TAKE THEM FOR GRANTED, WE DON'T STOP TO MAKE SURE THE TRAITS WE'RE ASSIGNING TO A GROUP (A CATEGORY OF PEOPLE) REALLY, TRULY, REPRESENT ALL THE MEMBERS OF THAT GROUP. I KNOW SOME REALLY LAZY NEGROES BUT I ALSO A LOT OF REALLY LAZY CAUCASIANS. THAT HAS NOTHING TO DO WITH EITHER CATEGORY - IT ONLY HAS TO DO WITH THE CATEGORY,'LAZY'. MAYBE PARSON WILL DO A SERMON ABOUT IT. I THINK I'LL LET HIM READ THIS ENTRY AND SEE WHAT HE THINKS. MAYBE HE WON'T PREACH ABOUT IT. ALL MINISTERS ARE PRETTY NARROW-MINDED, YOU KNOW! HA! HA! HA! SOMETIMES I JUST KILL MYSELF!!!!!

POSITIVE, SOCIAL, AGREEMENT # 17

I WILL look beyond categories, and make my decisions about people based on each individual's broad array of personal traits,

RATHER THAN first seeking to place a person within some broad category as my basis for understanding or evaluating him or her. (smart-dumb, male-female, black-white-yellow-brown, teen-adult, Christian-Moslem-Atheist, Lawyer-Clergyman, etc.)

BECAUSE a category can reflect only one of the hundreds of important traits people possess, so reacting to a person by any one category (trait), forces one to miss all the rest. (Are all whites, bigots? All teens, dope heads? All males, slovenly? All Christians, honest? All cheerleaders, social snobs?)

Topic Eighteen:
Focusing on solutions

AGE 5 [SECOND DAY OF GRADE ONE]
DEAR DIARY,
   I WONDER HOW GROWNUPS CAN BE SO STUPID. AFTER SCHOOL TODAY MALCOME AND I DID NOT GO RIGHT STRAIGHT HOME. WE WENT DOWN TO THE CREEK AND SKIPPED STONES AND CLIMBED TREES. WE PLANNED A ROPE SWING OUT OVER THE WATER FROM THE CHESTNUT TREE. WE STAYED TOO LONG (<u>WAY</u> TOO LONG I HAVE TO GUESS FROM THE WAY OUR PARENTS REACTED). I WALKED HIM TO HIS HOUSE BEFORE I WENT HOME. HIS MOTHER MET US IN THE FRONT YARD SCREAMING. SHE DRAGGED MALCOME UP TO THE PORCH STEPS AND BEGAN SPANKING HIM OVER AND OVER AND OVER AGAIN. HE SCREAMED AND KICKED AND I RAN HOME. IT WAS THE FIRST SPANKING I HAD EVER REALLY SEEN GIVEN. IT WAS TERRIBLE. WHEN I GOT HOME I WENT INSIDE THROUGH THE KITCHEN DOOR. I WAS PRETTY UPSET, I CAN TELL YOU THAT. MOM CAME TO ME AND HUGGED ME AND SAID, "WHERE ON EARTH HAVE YOU BEEN? WE'VE BEEN SO WORRIED." I TOLD HER, AND POP CAME INTO THE ROOM. HE SAID ABOUT THE SAME THING EXCEPT HE ENDED IT WITH, "SIT DOWN AT THE TABLE. WE HAVE TO TALK." THAT ALMOST ALWAYS MEANS A PROBLEM. THEY LET ME TELL THEM WHERE I HAD BEEN AND WHAT HAPPENED AT MALCOME'S. THEN THEY ASKED IF I HAD ANY IDEAS WHAT TIME IT WAS. I DIDN'T AND WAS AMAZED IT WAS ALMOST SIX. "I CAN SEE WHY YOU ARE WORRIED," I SAID TO THEM. MOM SAID, "WE SURE HAVE BEEN WORRIED. WHAT ARE YOU GOING TO DO ABOUT THINGS LIKE THIS?" I PUT MY CHIN ON MY FOLDED HANDS ON THE TABLE AND THOUGHT FOR A LONG TIME. THEY JUST SAT THERE QUIETLY - WHICH I APPRECIATED. I FIRST THOUGHT THAT IF I HAD A WATCH THAT WOULD HELP, BUT I KNEW IT WOULD BE TOO EXPENSIVE AND THAT I WOULD

CERTAINLY LOSE IT ANYWAY. (I LOSE THINGS!) FOR A MINUTE I CONSIDERED A HUGE BALL OF TWINE WITH ONE END TIED TO MY WAIST SO THEY COULD GIVE IT A TUG WHEN THEY WANTED ME. I COULD TELL THEY WERE WORRIED SICK AND I WAS VERY, VERY SORRY BUT I LEARNED BACK WHEN I WAS A LITTLE KID THAT SORRY IS GOOD BUT IT IS NEVER ENOUGH. THEN THE BEST ANSWER CAME TO ME. "I SHOULD ALWAYS TELL YOU WHERE I AM GOING BEFORE I GO THERE. I GUESS I JUST FIGURED SINCE I WAS A SCHOOLBOY NOW I DIDN'T HAVE TO DO THAT. I'M SORRY." ALL POP SAID WAS, "WE HAVE THAT DEAL, THEN, DO WE?" HE HELD OUT HIS HAND - POP IS BIG ON HAND SHAKES OVER REALLY IMPORTANT THINGS. "YES, SIR, WE HAVE THAT DEAL," I SAID AND I SHOOK HIS HAND A LITTLE LONGER THAN USUAL TO LET HIM KNOW I WAS VERY SINCERE. THEN MOM SAID, "WASH UP - SUPPER'S WAITING." I WILL NEVER HEAR ANYMORE ABOUT IT, DI. I KNOW THAT. IT IS ALL TAKEN CARE OF AS LONG AS I KEEP UP MY END OF IT - AND I WILL. AND I LEARNED SOMETHING I REALLY SHOULD HAVE ALREADY KNEW (OR KNOWN, MAYBE?). THE STUPID GROWN-UP PART OF ALL THIS WAS NOT MY MOM AND POP, IT WAS MALCOME'S MOTHER. SHE INTENTIONALLY HURT HER SON REALLY BAD. HE'LL BE SHOWING OFF HIS BRUISED BEHIND TO ALL THE GUYS TOMORROW. I'M SURE OF THAT. BUT (WHAT A GREAT PUN!) SHE DID NOT REALLY HELP HIM MAKE A PLAN TO KEEP IT FROM HAPPENING TOMORROW OR THE NEXT DAY. I WILL HAVE TO TALK TO HIM ABOUT SETTING A 'GO HOME FIRST' RULE FOR HIMSELF. SHE REALLY DIDN'T HELP HIM AND I SUPPOSE BY NOW SHE FEELS REALLY TERRIBLE ABOUT HURTING HER SON SO BADLY. SHE REALLY DID HURT HIM. YOU SEE - STUPID GROWN-UP STUFF. I DO NOT KNOW WHAT MORE TO SAY - STUPID GROWN-UP BEHAVIOR !!! (THAT 'BUT' THING WAS PRETTY FUNNY!)

AGE 6 1/2 [GRADE 3]

    DI - TEACHERS, MOST PARENTS, AND EVEN MR. MARTIN ARE REALLY STUPID WHEN IT COMES TO HELPING KIDS LEARN HOW TO KEEP FROM GETTING INTO TROUBLE. MY TEACHER TOLD BRENDA TO STAND IN THE CORNER BECAUSE SHE HAD STAYED IN THE RESTROOM TOO LONG. I RAISED MY HAND AND ASKED HOW THAT WAS GOING TO HELP HER LEARN HOW TO GET BACK TO THE ROOM MORE QUICKLY. MAYBE SHE NEEDS TO LEARN HOW TO WASH HER HANDS MORE QUICKLY. MAYBE SHE HAS A LOWER DIGESTIVE TRACT ILLNESS TODAY SO IT TOOK LONGER THAN USUAL. WOULDN'T IT MAKE MORE SENSE TO FIND OUT WHAT HAD GONE WRONG AND HELP HER FIX IT?
    I SPENT THE REST OF THE DAY WITH MR. MARTIN. HE TOLD ME TO GO TO THE DESK IN THE CORNER AND READ OR SOMETHING. I TOLD HIM I THOUGHT HE SHOULD GIVE ME A SPANKING LIKE HE GAVE JUNIOR LAST WEEK WHEN JUNIOR SPAT AT MARY ELLEN. I SAID, "IT CERTAINLY MAKES AS MUCH SENSE TO DO IT TO ME FOR SPEAKING UP AS IT DID FOR JUNIOR. IN NEITHER CASE WILL IT SHOW EITHER ONE OF US WHAT TO DO THE NEXT TIME WE BECOME FRUSTRATED ABOUT SOMETHING GOING ON IN THAT CLASSROOM, BUT IT SEEMS TO SOMEHOW BE THE THING SCHOOL PEOPLE THINK WILL MAGICALLY GIVE US THE INFORMATION." I WAS REALLY STEAMED AND GOT MORE STEAMED THE MORE I TALKED. HE JUST SAID THAT MAKING THE RULES AT THE SCHOOL WAS NOT MY BUSINESS AND THAT HE WOULD DEAL WITH ME AND WITH JUNIOR IN THE WAYS HE DECIDED WAS BEST. I GOT IN ONE MORE REMARK BEFORE HE CARRIED ME OVER TO THE CHAIR. "SCHOOL PEOPLE ARE SUPPOSED TO KNOW HOW TO HELP KIDS LEARN, NOT HURT THEM FOR WHAT THEY HAVE NOT LEARNED WELL ENOUGH YET." MR. MARTIN WAS NOT HIS USUAL CHATTY SELF TODAY. PERHAPS THERE ARE PROBLEMS AT HOME.

POSITIVE, SOCIAL, AGREEMENT # 18

I WILL, when I, an acquaintance, or someone under my supervision makes an error or behaves dangerously or irresponsibly, approach it as a problem needing solving and attempt to provide the necessary information, training or resources so it will not need to occur again

RATHER THAN first placing blame followed by punishment,

BECAUSE blame and punishment provide no useful guidelines to enable one to make the necessary changes. To hurt another person in order to induce positive change has been shown throughout history (and in laboratories) to be a false assumption that leads to social collapse. Punishment is typically utilized by those who themselves are unable or unwilling to provide appropriate training methods.

Topic Nineteen:
Basing decisions on verifiable facts

AGE 9 [GRADE 8]

DI - I'VE DISCOVERED SOMETHING THAT IS MORE DEVASTATING TO HUMANITY THAN IGNORANCE - <u>THE WILLINGNESS TO REMAIN IGNORANT</u>. BY IGNORANCE I DON'T MEAN BEING A SLOW LEARNER, I MEAN NOT HAVING THE REQUIRED OR NECESSARY INFORMATION ABOUT SOMETHING. SOMETIMES WE ARE IGNORANT BECAUSE SOME PIECE OF INFORMATION IS NOT AVAILABLE - LIKE THE CURE FOR POLIO OR THE DIMENSIONS OF THE UNIVERSE. WE CAN'T HELP THAT. BUT SOME PEOPLE DON'T WANT TO KNOW THE REAL REASONS FOR THINGS OR THE REAL FACTS -THEY CHOOSE TO REMAIN IGNORANT AND THAT STEAMS ME, I'LL TELL YOU THAT!!! BUTCHIE'S DAD BEATS HIM SO BADLY THAT SOME DAYS HE CAN'T EVEN COME TO SCHOOL. THIS AFTERNOON I TRIED TO EXPLAIN TO HIS DAD THAT BEATING HAS BEEN PROVED TO BE INEFFECTIVE IN LONG-TERM BEHAVIOR CHANGE AND I EVEN TOOK HIM A BOOK BY DR. STONE - A PSYCHOLOGIST - THAT SHOWED BETTER, PROVEN WAYS TO HELP CHILDREN BEHAVE BETTER. HE SWORE AT ME, THREW THE BOOK AGAINST THE WALL AND SLAPPED BUTCHIE SO HARD IT KNOCKED HIM AGAINST THE WALL AND ONTO THE FLOOR. HE SPOKE GIBBERISH, BUT THE ESSENCE WAS: "I'LL BEAT HIM IF I THINK THAT'S BEST. NOW GET OUT OF MY LIFE FOREVER AND TAKE YOUR FANCY DOCTORS ADVICE WITH YOU." (AND THE SOCIAL WORKERS THINK <u>I</u> SHOULD BE REMOVED FROM <u>MY</u> HOME?). FACTS, INFORMATION, SCIENCE - NONE OF IT HAD ANY IMPACT BECAUSE HE WANTED TO REMAIN IGNORANT. ALL I SUCCEEDED IN DOING WAS TO GET BUTCHIE'S HEAD BASHED IN. THE MAN IS MAKING IMPORTANT DECISIONS FOR BUTCHIE EVERYDAY THAT ARE BASED ON DANGEROUS IGNORANCE. I DON'T KNOW FOR SURE HOW TO COMBAT THAT WHEN A PERSON IS SO

HELL-BENT (EXCUSE!) ON REMAINING IGNORANT. I FEEL SO HELPLESS. I THINK I'M GOING TO BE SICK TO MY STOMACH.
[I WAS AND AM! LATER IN LIFE I SPENT FIVE YEARS RESEARCHING THIS MENTALITY BY LIVING AMONG IT AND WROTE ABOUT IT IN, *CRISIS OF MYTHS*.]

AGE 6 ½ [GRADE THREE]
SOMETIMES, DI, EVEN WHEN A GUY TRIES TO DO THE RIGHT THING, HE (I) GETS INTO TROUBLE. EVER SINCE GINNY AND I HAVE BEEN LITTLE KIDS WE'VE SNEAKED OFF TO THE CREEK AND GONE SKINNY DIPPING. WELL, EARLY IN THE SUMMER HER MOTHER FOUND OUT AND TOLD GINNY SHE WAS TOO BIG A GIRL TO GO SKINNY DIPPING AND SHE'D HAVE TO WEAR A SUIT. I THINK IT'S A DUMB RULE BUT I NEVER EVER TRIED TO TALK HER OUT OF IT. I DON'T CARE WHAT SHE WEARS OR DOESN'T WEAR. SO, TODAY WE WENT DOWN TO THE CREEK AND SHE WORE HER SWIMSUIT JUST LIKE THE NEW RULE SAYS. SINCE NOBODY HAD GIVEN ME SUCH A RULE I JUST SWAM IN MY BIRTHDAY SUIT LIKE USUAL. IT ALL SEEMED FINE TO BOTH OF US. WELL, GINNY'S BROTHER FOUND US AND GOT REAL MAD AT ME. I COULDN'T SEE WHERE I'D DONE ANYTHING WRONG AND NEITHER COULD GINNY. WELL, I GOT LECTURES FROM HER BROTHER, HER MOM, MY MOM, MY POP, AND I FULLY EXPECT I'LL GET ANOTHER FROM PARSON IN THE NEAR FUTURE. I JUST DON'T GET WHAT I DID WRONG. I FOLLOWED GINNY'S RULE EXACTLY. IT APPEARS THAT GROWN UPS HAVE A BIG SERIOUS THING ABOUT NAKEDNESS AND EVEN THOUGH GINNY AND I KNOW ALL ABOUT HOW EACH LOOKS NAKED, SUDDENLY WE HAVE TO KEEP OUR SPECIAL PARTS COVERED UP AS IF THEY WERE BIG SECRETS. SURE SEEMS ABSURD. I CAN SKINNY DIP WITH THE GUYS BUT JUST NOT WITH GIRLS. I REALLY DON'T GET IT BUT IF THAT'S THE NEW RULE I GUESS GINNY AND I WILL JUST CLIMB TREES INSTEAD OF GOING SWIMMING. THE THING THAT BOTHERS ME IS

THAT ALL THE GROWN-UPS SEEM TO THINK WE WERE DOING SOME TERRIBLE THING. WE'RE SIX, FOR GOSH SAKE! WHAT TERRIBLE THING COULD WE POSSIBLY DO? THEY JUST DON'T UNDERSTAND. I HAVE THE FEELING IT'S ALL CONNECTED TO THE WAY GROWN-UPS GO ABOUT MAKING BABIES. I'LL HAVE TO TALK WITH DOC ABOUT IT. ALL I KNOW IS THE GROWN-UPS USED UP A WHOLE LOT MORE EMOTION AND ENERGY THAN SEEMS REASONABLE. MAYBE IF I'D HAVE KIDNAPPED HER I COULD UNDERSTAND HOW UPSET THEY WERE BUT . . . I'M SURE IT MUST BE RELATED TO SOMETHING THEY ARE ALL ASHAMED OF. IT JUST DOESN'T SEEM RIGHT THAT A PERSON IS SUPPOSED TO BE ASHAMED OF HIS BODY BUT I'M PRETTY SURE THAT'S WHAT'S AT THE BOTTOM OF ALL THIS.

AGE 5 ½ [GRADE ONE]
DEAR DIARY,
 THIS WAS MY FIRST DAY OF SCHOOL. WE STARTED AT 8:30. AT 9:00 I GOT TO MEET THE PRINCIPAL, MR. MARTIN. I'M NOT SURE WHY I UPSET MY TEACHER SO MUCH BUT MR. MARTIN SAID I SHOULDN'T WORRY. HE TALKED TO HER FIRST AND THEN HE ASKED ME INTO HIS OFFICE - A PRETTY PLEASANT PLACE WITH LOTS OF BOOKS - AND HE ASKED ME WHAT I THOUGHT HAD HAPPENED. THAT WAS PRETTY NICE I THOUGHT. HE TRIED TO SEE ALL SIDES OF IT BEFORE HE DID ANYTHING. IT STARTED WHEN MRS. STAR WAS CALLED TO THE PHONE ABOUT HER SICK FATHER. SHE LOOKED AROUND THE ROOM AND SAID, "CRAIGY, YOU'RE IN CHARGE UNTIL I GET BACK. IF ANYBODY ACTS UP YOU'LL TELL ME." I COULD TELL THEY WERE ALL GETTING RESTLESS EVEN BEFORE SHE HAD SAID ANYTHING - NONE OF US HAD EVER BEEN CORRALLED INTO CHAIRS AND DESKS BEFORE AND EXPECTED TO JUST

SIT STILL. (A REALLY DUMB ARRANGEMENT, BY THE WAY.) SO, I HAD ALL THE KIDS GO TO THE LIBRARY CORNER AND SIT ON THE FLOOR WHILE I READ PETER PAN TO THEM. THEY WERE QUIET AND VERY WELL BEHAVED TO MY WAY OF THINKING AND I HAD THOUGHT ABOUT THE VERY GOOD REPORT I WOULD BE ABLE TO GIVE TO THE TEACHER WHEN SHE CAME BACK. THE KIDS SEEMED INTERESTED IN THE STORY (I SORT OF ACTED IT OUT WHILE I READ). THEN MRS. STAR CAME BACK AND STARTED SCREAMING ABOUT US BEING ON THE FLOOR AND OUT OF OUR SEATS AND SHE TOOK ME BY THE COLLAR DOWN TO MR. MARTIN'S OFFICE. ON THE WAY I TOLD HER I WAS SORRY SHE WAS SO UPSET AND THAT I FIGURED IT HAD SOMETHING TO DO WITH THE TENSION ABOUT HER FATHER'S ILLNESS. AT THAT POINT SHE LET GO OF MY COLLAR AND TOOK ME BY THE EAR THE REST OF THE WAY. AT THE END OF MY PRIVATE TALK WITH MR. MARTIN I SUGGESTED SHE MAY NEED SOME TIME OFF UNTIL HER FAMILY PROBLEMS GET SOLVED. HE SMILED AT ME AND SAID SOMETHING VERY NICE. "CRAIGY, I THINK WE ARE GOING TO GET TO KNOW EACH OTHER VERY WELL DURING THE NEXT FEW YEARS."

    I THOUGHT THAT WAS VERY FRIENDLY OF HIM. BUT THE POINT OF ALL THIS IS THAT HE TOOK THE TIME TO FIND OUT WHAT HAD HAPPENED AND WHAT I WAS TRYING TO DO. MRS. STAR DIDN'T. SHE DIDN'T ONCE ASK ME WHAT WAS GOING ON. SHE DIDN'T TAKE THE TIME TO JUST TO WATCH AT FIRST AND SEE WHAT WAS REALLY GOING ON. SHE JUST FELL APART IN FRONT OF THE WHOLE FIRST GRADE AND GOD. I FEEL BAD FOR HER. PEOPLE WHO JUMP TO CONCLUSIONS ALWAYS SEEM TO BE UNLIKABLE PEOPLE. I WONDER IF SHE HAS ANY FRIENDS? I HOPE SO.

POSITIVE, SOCIAL, AGREEMENT # 19

I WILL gather the necessary facts and information (listen and study) before rendering decisions, opinions or judgments

RATHER THAN making snap judgments and decisions or offering opinions based on ignorance,

BECAUSE only through accurate information can appropriately helpful actions be formulated and implemented.

Topic Twenty: Respecting possessions

Topic Twenty
Respecting possessions

AGE 7 ½ [GRADE FIVE]
DI -
    PARSON POSED AN INTERESTING QUESTION IN HIS SERMON THIS MORNING AND I CONGRATULATED HIM ON IT. HE WAS TALKING ABOUT WORLDLY POSSESSIONS (I AM NOT SURE HOW YOU COULD HAVE A POSSESSION THAT WASN'T, WORLDLY, BUT I LET THAT SLIP BY). HE ASKED, "IF YOU COULD ONLY KEEP 12 OF YOUR 'WORLDLY" POSSESSIONS (BESIDES YOUR CLOTHES. NAKEDNESS - NAMELY THE LACK THEREOF - AGAIN REARS ITS STRANGE, PROTESTANT, HEAD??? - 'REARS' - THAT'S HILARIOUS!) - WHAT WOULD THEY BE?" ISN'T THAT A FASCINATING QUESTION, DI? PARSON ASSUMED ONE OF THOSE THINGS WOULD BE A BIBLE, BUT SINCE I PRETTY WELL HAVE THAT MEMORIZED, I FIGURE I'LL SKIP THAT. HERE IS MY LIST SO FAR: 1 - A BOOK OF THOREAU'S ESSAYS WHICH INCLUDES WALDON POND, 2 - A COLLECTION OF EMERSON'S WRITINGS, 3 - THE TWO-VOLUME SET OF THE LINCOLN LIBRARY - IT PRETTY WELL SUMMARIZES MOST OF MAN'S KNOWLEDGE [AND IN 1944 IT WAS STILL ACTUALLY ABLE TO DO JUST THAT!], (THOSE FIRST THREE THINGS WOULD MOSTLY BE FOR ME TO PASS ON TO MY CHILDREN SOME DAY) 4 - I'D KEEP THE AMERICAN FLAG THAT MOM MADE FOR ME BY HAND, 5 - AND THE JACKKNIFE POP GAVE ME FOR MY 7TH BIRTHDAY, 6 - MY BLUE AND RED BIKE, ALTHOUGH I COULD ALWAYS MAKE ANOTHER ONE IF THAT WERE ALLOWED, 7 - I'D KEEP YOU DI - TO SEE WHERE I'VE BEEN IN THIS LIFE. I'M STUMPED ABOUT WHAT ELSE I'D KEEP. I GUESS THERE REALLY ISN'T MUCH I NEED, IS THERE? I'D PROBABLY KEEP A RADIO AS NUMBER 8. I WONDER, IF I'D KEEP MY LIBRARY CARD, IF I COULD DELETE THE THREE BOOKS ENTRIES? I WONDER IF I COULD KEEP ONE BOX WHICH CONTAINED 10,000 BABY RUTH CANDY BARS? NOW I'M JUST GETTING SILLY. IT REALLY IS A GOOD MENTAL EXERCISE. I AM THANKFUL PARSON FINALLY PREACHED ABOUT SOMETHING WORTHWHILE. (THAT IS NOT EXACTLY HOW I PUT IT TO

HIM, HOWEVER!)

AGE 8 ½ [GRADE SEVEN]
 DI - I'VE SAID IT HERE BEFORE, DI, I REALLY FEEL SORRY FOR BUTCHIE. HE'S A BULLY. HE HURTS PEOPLE AND HE STEALS ALL KIND OF THINGS. WHENEVER ANYTHING IS MISSING HERE IN SPRINGTOWN, OFFICER HOEFFER JUST GOES OVER TO BUTCHIES'S PLACE AND FINDS IT. BUTCHIE IS NEVER 'SURE' HOW IT GOT THERE AND HIS DAD SWEARS (WELL, HE SWEARS A <u>LOT</u>, BUT IT'S A FIGURE OF SPEECH HERE) THAT THE KIDS BRING THE STUFF OVER TO GET HIS SON IN TROUBLE. HIS DAD HAS BEEN IN JAIL FOR ROBBERY MORE THAN ONCE, HIMSELF. I WONDER IF IT'S IN THE GENES OR IN THE FAMILY VALUES - I'M PRETTY SURE ABOUT THE VALUES SIDE OF IT AT LEAST. NONE OF THEM RESPECTS OTHER PEOPLE'S PROPERTY. (I FORGET IF 'NONE' IS SINGULAR OR PLURAL?) BUTCHIE DOESN'T EVEN SEEM TO RESPECT HIS OWN PROPERTY - HE BANGS HOLES IN THE WALLS OF HIS OWN HOUSE AND BREAKS HIS FURNITURE AND I'M PRETTY SURE HE KILLED HIS MOTHER'S CAT - DR. FREUD WOULD HAVE A FIELD DAY WITH THAT! I ALWAYS FIGURED I'D NOT WANT ANYBODY TO TAKE OR DAMAGE MY STUFF SO IT WOULDN'T BE FAIR (REASONABLE) FOR ME TO TAKE OR DAMAGE ANYBODY ELSE'S. WHAT DO YOU SUPPOSE IS EVER GOING TO HAPPEN TO BUTCHIE, DI? I'LL BET HE MAKES LIFE MISERABLE FOR A LOT OF PEOPLE WHEN HE GROWS UP.
 [Butchie was killed in a bank robbery attempt when he was nineteen. His father was seriously injured in the same incident.]

POSITIVE, SOCIAL, AGREEMENT # 20

I WILL keep only to my own rightful possessions,

RATHER THAN molesting or taking that which is not legitimately mine,

BECAUSE each person has the right to retain what he or she has earned or been given.

Topic Twenty-one:
Responsible provision for oneself and dependants

AGE 7 ½ [GRADE FIVE]

WELL, DI, I JUST HAD A STRANGE EXPERIENCE - MAYBE ENLIGHTENING OR STARTLING OR EDUCATIONAL EXPERIENCE WOULD BE BETTER TERMS. ANY WAY, IT WAS A VERY HOT AND HUMID NIGHT LAST NIGHT, SO I GOT UP EARLY TO GO DOWN TO THE CREEK FOR A SKINNY DIP TO COOL OFF AND THINK LIKE I OFTEN DO. WELL, WHEN I GOT TO THE PLACE I LIKE TO SWIM, I JUST AUTOMATICALLY SHED MY PINSTRIPES. IT WAS THEN I REALIZED THAT GINNY'S OLDER BROTHER, TOM, WAS ALREADY THERE SKINNY DIPPING WITH A GIRL (WHO I WILL NOT NAME TO PROTECT HER REPUTATION). SHE WAS JUST COMING OUT OF THE WATER AND WE STOOD THERE BARE NAKED LOOKING AT EACH OTHER WHILE TOM LAUGHED HIS HEAD OFF IN THE WATER. (NOW I'M PRETTY SURE I UNDERSTAND ABOUT THE GIRL'S BUMPY SWEATERS - POOR THINGS.) WELL, I WAS TOO SURPRISED TO BE EMBARRASSED (PLUS I AM SEVEN AND I'VE YET TO MEET A SEVEN-YEAR OLD BOY WHO FEELS THE NEED TO BE MODEST OR EMBARRASSED ABOUT SUCH THINGS.) SHE SCRAMBLED INTO HER CLOTHES AND LEFT. I DIDN'T WATCH HER GET DRESSED THOUGH I COULD SEE THAT TOM DID. WHEN SHE WAS GONE HE MOTIONED ME INTO THE WATER. HE WAS STILL LAUGHING. I DON'T THINK THE GIRL EVEN KNEW HOW TO SWIM SO I SUSPECT THERE HAD BEEN SOME HANKY-PANKY TAKING PLACE INSTEAD (THOUGH I'M NOT ENTIRELY SURE WHAT TAKES PLACE DURING HANKY-PANKY AND I GET THE IDEA I'M NOT SUPPOSED TO ASK ABOUT IT UNTIL I TURN THIRTEEN OR SO.) TOM AND I HAD A GOOD TIME - IT WAS THE FIRST TIME HE AND I EVER JUST DID SOMETHING TOGETHER - THE TWO OF US. HE'S LIKE A BIG, HAIRY, SEVEN YEAR OLD. I ASKED HIM IF HE WAS GOING TO MARRY THE GIRL - SEEING AS HE HAD SEEN HER NAKED. HE SAID HE NEVER

PLANNED ON GETTING MARRIED. HE SAID WHEN I GOT OLDER I'D LEARN THAT GIRLS WERE JUST PLAYTHINGS AND NOT TO GET EMOTIONALLY INVOLVED WITH THEM. NOT YET HAVING BEEN EMOTIONALLY INVOLVED WITH ANYTHING, SO FAR AS I CAN TELL, I'M NOT REALLY SURE WHAT HE MEANT. I ASKED HIM IF HE LOVED HER AND HE LAUGHED OUT LOUD AND SNORTED, "NO! NEVER!" I WANTED TO TELL HIM IT WAS WRONG TO BE NAKED WITH GIRLS BUT I FIGURED HE KNEW THAT ALREADY. I ASKED HIM IF HE HAD A JOB THESE DAYS. HE SAID JOBS ARE LIKE THE PLAGUE - TO BE AVOIDED AT ALL COSTS. I ASKED HIM WHY HE DIDN'T WANT TO SUPPORT HIMSELF LIKE OTHER GUYS HIS AGE DID. HE JUST ASKED, "WHY WOULD I WANT TO DO THAT! DAD AND MOM ARE STILL GOOD FOR IT (THIS, FROM A 24 YEAR OLD MAN!) I ASKED, "ISN'T THAT LIKE TAKING WHAT'S NOT REALLY YOURS?" HE SAID, "I DIDN'T ASK TO BE BORN. IT'S ALL THEIR DOING SO THEY [PARENTS] CAN JUST SUPPORT ME." I FELT SO SORRY FOR HIM - A GROWN MAN AND HE HAS NO SKILLS AT ALL (EXCEPT HANKY-PANKYING, I PRESUME). I DID ASK HIM ONE WEIGHTY QUESTION WHICH WAS REALLY NOT MY PLACE. I ASKED, "WHAT IF EVERYBODY TOOK YOUR ATTITUDE? THE WORLD WOULD FALL APART." HE JUST SHRUGGED HIS SHOULDERS AND DIDN'T ATTEMPT AN ANSWER - HE DUNKED ME INSTEAD. THE TALKING WAS UPSETTING BUT THE SWIMMING WAS GREAT. I THINK I WOULD HAVE BEEN A BETTER BIG BROTHER THAN TOM IS - NOT BRAGGING OR ANYTHING - BUT <u>HE</u> IS REALLY A LOUSY MODEL.

AGE 9 ½ [GRADE NINE, 1946]
    DI - MOM AND POP NEVER INCLUDE ME IN THEIR TALKS ABOUT MONEY AND THAT'S OKAY. I SUPPOSE IT IS THEIR BUSINESS AS THE PARENTS. I KNOW POP GETS A MONTHLY CHECK FROM THE PLANT HE WORKED AT ALL THOSE YEARS. I SAW IT ONCE BY ACCIDENT. IT WAS FROM THE 'DISABILITY FUND" AND WAS FOR $42.53. IF HE

WORKED 40 HOURS A WEEK FOR THAT IT WOULD BE LIKE 28 CENTS AN HOUR WHICH IS NOT TOO BAD CONSIDERING HE NEVER FINISHED GRADE SCHOOL. I DON'T THINK OF HIM AS DISABLED BUT HE DOES HAVE A LUNG DISEASE HE GOT AT THE PLANT FROM WORKING IN THE CUTTING ROOM, SO THAT'S PROBABLY WHAT IT REFERRED TO. I FIGURE MOM HAS 25 FAMILIES SHE WASHES AND IRONS FOR SO I'D GUESS SHE BRINGS IN CLOSE TO $100 A MONTH. THE HOUSE IS PAID FOR - POP NEVER MISSES A CHANCE TO MENTION THAT. HE'S REALLY PROUD THAT HE OWNS IT. I THINK THAT IS CONNECTED TO THE FACT THAT HE WAS THE FIRST MALE CHILD BORN A FREE MAN IN HIS FAMILY AND OWNING A HOUSE SORT OF PROVES THAT FOR ALL TO SEE. I THINK THAT ALL TOGETHER THEY EARN ABOUT $1700 A YEAR. BILLY SAYS HIS DAD EARNS $3500 A YEAR AS PLANT SUPERVISOR AND JOHN'S DAD MAKES $4500 BECAUSE HE OWNS THE BLUE AND WHITE GROCERY STORES HERE AND OVER IN GOSHEN. OUR INCOME COMES TO ABOUT $4.70 A DAY AND OF COURSE 20% OF THAT (.94) GOES TO THE CHARITY JAR AND 10% (.47) GOES INTO THE SAVING ACCOUNT SO THAT LEAVES US $3.29 TO LIVE ON. IT AMAZES ME, DI, HOW WELL YOU CAN LIVE THESE DAYS ON $1.10 APIECE A DAY. I WONDER WHAT BILLY'S FOLKS DO WITH ALL THEIR EXTRA MONEY. PARSON ONCE LET IT SLIP TO ME THAT MY PARENTS WERE THE POOREST (MONEY-WISE) COUPLE IN TOWN. (HE WAS TRYING TO MAKE THE POINT THAT THEY WERE ONLY MONEY-POOR AND NOT POOR IN THE WAYS THAT REALLY COUNT - AS IF I HAVE NOT KNOWN THAT SINCE BEFORE I TURNED FIVE!). WELL, I DID ALL THIS FIGURING, DI, BECAUSE NOW MY MAIL-ORDER, PERSONALIZED PENCIL BUSINESS IS MAKING THE FAMILY A LOT OF MONEY ($22.50 PROFIT LAST WEEK ALONE AND THAT WAS A SLOW WEEK.) MY JOB AT GOLDSMITH'S HARDWARE TAKES TEN HOURS A WEEK WHICH BRINGS IN ANOTHER $3.00 SO I ESTIMATE I'M NOW MAKING ABOUT AS MUCH AS MOM. IT ALL GOES INTO THE FAMILY

ACCOUNT, OF COURSE, AND POP HAS STARTED GIVING ME AN ALLOWANCE OF FIFTY CENTS A WEEK - THAT'S A VERY GOOD ALLOWANCE IN THIS TOWN. I KNOW THEY PUT MY MONEY INTO A COLLEGE SAVING ACCOUNT. DOC SAYS I'LL GET A FULL SCHOLARSHIP TO COLLEGE SO I WISH THEY WOULD USE MORE OF MY INCOME FOR THEMSELVES - BUT THEN, I CAN'T IMAGINE WHAT THEY'D USE IT FOR. I FIGURE MOM COULD CUT BACK ON THE NUMBER OF WASHES SHE DOES. THAT WOULD BE GOOD. I AM TRYING TO MUSTER THE COURAGE - NO, IT'S MORE JUST TRYING TO FIND THE RIGHT APPROACH TO TALK WITH MOM AND POP ABOUT THAT. POP IS A VERY PROUD MAN. I KNOW IT HURTS HIM AWFULLY INSIDE THAT HE HAS NOT BEEN ABLE TO WORK AND FULLY SUPPORT US, BUT HE'S 69 YEARS OLD! MOST GUYS SLOW WAY DOWN WHEN THEY REACH THAT OLD AN AGE - MANY HAVE SLOWED DOWN COMPLETELY - HA! HA!). POP IS ALSO PROUD THAT HE STILL HAS A FULL HEAD OF HAIR THOUGH I DON'T BELIEVE BALDNESS RUNS IN MOST NEGRO FAMILY BLOODLINES. (I'LL HAVE TO ASK DOC.) I AM SO LUCKY TO BE A FRANKLIN.

POSITIVE, SOCIAL, AGREEMENT # 21

I WILL, to the best of my ability, provide for myself and those dependant upon me (realizing this is a gradual process based on maturation),

RATHER THAN being dependant upon others beyond what is reasonable, considering any defensible limitations I may be unable to overcome or work around,

BECAUSE in a truly humanity-friendly society, everyone shares responsibilities to the limits of their potential.

Topic Twenty-two:
Remaining curious about people and their differences

AGE 5 [GRADE ONE]
DEAR DIARY,
    BILLY AND I SLEPT OVER AT JOHNS LAST NIGHT. IT WAS MY FIRST SEVERAL PERSON SLEEP OVER. YOU LEARN INTERESTING THINGS ABOUT OTHER PEOPLE AT A SLEEP OVER. JOHN IS AFRAID OF THE DARK AND BILLY WORRIES ABOUT TROLLS UNDER THE BED. JOHN SLEEPS IN PAJAMAS OVER HIS UNDER WARE. BILLY JUST SLEEPS IN HIS UNDER WARE AND, OF COURSE, I JUST SLEEP IN MY SKIN. I TRIED JOHNS PJ'S AND HE TRIED IT NAKED BUT NEITHER OF US FELT COMFORTABLE SO WE DECIDED TO TRADE BACK (WELL, I GAVE HIM HIS PJ'S BACK BUT I TOLD HIM HE COULDN'T HAVE MY SKIN - WE CRACKED UP OVER THAT ONE!). JOHNS PARENTS DON'T LISTEN TO PRAYERS AT NIGHT. MINE WOULD NEVER MISS THAT. BILLY CAN'T DRINK AFTER SIX O'CLOCK OR HE WETS THE BED. I NEVER CONSIDERED THAT MIGHT BE A PROBLEM. I THINK I COULD DESIGN A BALLOON HE COULD FASTEN ON HIMSELF SO IF HE WENT AT NIGHT IT WOULD GO INTO THE BALLOON. I WILL PERSONALLY TRY IT BEFORE I RECOMMEND IT TO HIM. JOHNS FOLKS LET HIM EAT IN HIS ROOM. I HAVE NEVER BEEN ALLOWED TO DO THAT - WELL, A BABY RUTH NOW AND THEN BUT NOT REGULARLY. THEY HAVE HOT WATER RIGHT OUT OF THE SPIGOT. THAT IS REALLY PRETTY HANDY. WE TOOK A BATH TOGETHER AND WHEN THE WATER STARTED GETTING COOL, JOHN JUST TURNED ON MORE HOT WATER AND IT WAS SOON JUST RIGHT AGAIN. PEOPLE ARE VERY DIFFERENT, DI, BUT THAT'S OKAY. DIFFERENT IS NOT BAD, IT IS JUST DIFFERENT. I THINK W E GET COMFORTABLE WITH WHAT WE ARE USED TO. I ALSO THINK SOME PEOPLE GET UNCOMFORTABLE AROUND WHAT THEY ARE NOT USED TO.

AGE 8 ½ SATURDAY AT 6:30 AM [GRADE SEVEN]

      DI - WE HAVE A NEW FAMILY IN TOWN - WELL A NEW COUPLE - THEY DON'T HAVE KIDS BUT I SUPPOSE THAT STILL QUALIFIES AS A FAMILY. I NEVER THOUGHT ABOUT THAT BEFORE. ANYWAY, THEIR LAST NAME IS GOLDSMITH - HIS FIRST NAME IS HARRY AND HERS IS SYLVIA. THEY LOOK TO BE IN THEIR FIFTIES SO I DOUBT IF THEY WILL START HAVING KIDS. MR. GOLDSMITH BOUGHT THE HARDWARE STORE. THE MEN AT THE FEED STORE SAY THEY ARE JEWS. (I'M NOT SURE IF IT'S RESPECTFUL TO CALL THEM JEWS OR IF I SHOULD SAY 'JEWISH PEOPLE'. MAYBE PARSON WILL KNOW. - THAT'S DUMB, CRAIGY. JUST ASK MR. GOLDSMITH.) THE MEN WEREN'T VERY COMPLEMENTARY ABOUT JEWS (I'LL USE THAT 'TIL I FIND OUT FOR SURE). THINGS LIKE BIG NOSES, BULGING BILLFOLDS, MONEY GRUBBERS (A STRANGE TERM). I DON'T KNOW HOW ANY OF THEM KNOW ANY OF THAT SINCE THESE ARE THE FIRST JEWS THAT EVER LIVED HERE AND MOST OF THE FEED STORE REGULARS HAVEN'T EVER BEEN FURTHER THAN GOSHEN. I LOOKED UP JUDAISM IN THE ENCYCLOPEDIA. THEY DON'T BELIEVE IN JESUS BUT THEY SEEM TO BELIEVE IN THE SAME GOD CHRISTIANS DO. THE TWO RELIGIONS SEEM TO SHARE THE SAME OLD TESTAMENT - WELL, MOSTLY. JEWS HAVE BEEN AROUND FOR MANY CENTURIES LONGER THAN CHRISTIANS SO MAYBE THEY KNOW SOME THINGS CHRISTIANS DON'T. AS FAR AS I CAN ASCERTAIN, THE STORY ABOUT JESUS SAYS HE WAS A JEW HIS WHOLE LIFE. WELL, I'M GOING OVER TO WELCOME THEM (THE GOLDSMITHS) TO SPRINGTOWN. HE OPENS THE STORE AT EIGHT SO I FIGURE THEY'LL BE UP AND AROUND BY 7:30. MOM'S MAKING RYE BREAD FOR THEM. I'VE BEEN SMELLING IT EVER SINCE I WOKE UP. THE AROMA OF BAKING BREAD IS LIKE THE 8TH WONDER OF THE WORLD (WONDER BREAD HA! HA!) MORE LATER.

10:30 AM

    WELL, DI - THERE WERE NO BIG NOSES AND NO BULGING WALLETS, I'LL TELL YOU THAT FOR SURE. THEY ARE LIKE REAL PEOPLE AS FAR AS I CAN TELL. THEY INVITED ME RIGHT IN AND INSISTED ON CUTTING THE BREAD AND SHARING IT WITH ME. THEY SEEM TO EAT THE SAME FOODS WE DO. SHE SQUEEZED FRESH ORANGE JUICE JUST FOR ME. WE SAT AT THE KITCHEN TABLE JUST LIKE HERE AT HOME. MR. GOLDSMITH - HE TOLD ME TO CALL HIM HARRY BUT I TOLD HIM I'D HAVE TO CHECK WITH MOM AND POP TO BE SURE THAT WOULD BE OKAY - HE KNEW ABOUT MY FIRST MOTHER AND FATHER - SINCE FATHER HAD WORKED IN THE HARDWARE STORE FOR A TIME, I GUESS. IT IS PROBABLY IN THE RECORDS. THEY BOTH SEEMED VERY INTERESTED IN ME. THEY MADE ME FEEL GOOD. HER GRAPE JAM WAS VERY GOOD. I MENTIONED IT AND SHE INSISTED ON SENDING A JAR HOME WITH ME. MR. GOLDSMITH SAID IF I WANTED TO EARN EXTRA MONEY HE NEEDED A FLOOR SWEEPER JUST BEFORE CLOSING EVERY AFTERNOON. I SAID I'D CHECK WITH MOM AND POP. I CAN SEE I'M GOING TO LIKE THEM A LOT. THE SAD PART IS, DI, THAT THE MEN AT THE FEED STORE ARE PROBABLY GOING TO MISS OUT ON GETTING TO HAVE SOME GOOD NEW FRIENDS BECAUSE THEY CAN'T SEE BEYOND THEIR OWN BIG NOSES - BEYOND THE WORD JEW (WHICH, BY THE WAY, THEY SEEM TO REALLY MISUNDERSTAND, BUT I WILL TRY TO CORRECT THAT LATER IN THE WEEK.).

    HARRY (POP SAYS THAT'S OKAY EXCEPT IN FORMAL SETTINGS) SAYS THE TERM JEW IS FINE - SYLVIA SAID TO JUST USE IT LIKE THE TERM BAPTIST OR METHODIST. WHAT WAS REALLY GREAT WAS WHEN SYLVIA THANKED ME FOR ASKING ABOUT THE TERM. I CAN TELL, I'LL BE HAVING LOTS OF EARLY MORNING BREAKFASTS IN THEIR KITCHEN. WHEN I LEFT, I WHISPERED TO HARRY OUT ON THE PORCH THAT I HAD BEEN CIRCUMCISED, TOO. I THOUGHT THAT MIGHT MAKE HIM FEEL MORE AT HOME.

AGE 8 ½ [GRADE SEVEN]

DI - I'VE WRITTEN ABOUT THE MOUNTAIN MAN BEFORE - ARNIE. HE IS SO BIG AND THE STORIES ABOUT HIM ARE SO BAD THAT I'VE ALWAYS BEEN SCARED TO APPROACH HIM. AFTER MY GOOD EXPERIENCE WITH THE GOLDSMITHS I FIGURED I PROBABLY NEED TO DO THE SAME WITH ARNIE - GET TO KNOW HIM MYSELF, I MEAN, AND NOT JUST BELIEVE WHAT THE FOLKS IN TOWN SAY ABOUT HIM. I ASKED POP WHAT HE THOUGHT. FOR SOME REASON HIS EYES SPARKLED. THAT ALWAYS MEANS HE KNOWS SOMETHING I DON'T. ANYWAY, I ASKED HIM BECAUSE I FIGURED I'D NEED HIS PERMISSION - CONSIDERING ARNIE'S REPUTATION. I'D NOT WANT TO PUT MYSELF IN DANGER. HE SAID, "GO FOR IT, SON." THE PROBLEM IS, HE (ARNIE) ONLY COMES INTO TOWN A FEW TIMES A YEAR, USUALLY TO SELL HIS PELTS. I'LL KEEP AN EYE OUT FOR HIM. I'LL BET I COULD LEARN A MILLION NEW THINGS FROM HIM. MAYBE I CAN HELP _HIM_ LEARN ABOUT TAKING BATHS. I HAVE BEEN CLOSE ENOUGH TO HIM TO KNOW HE SMELLS WORSE THAN HIS MULES.

[READ, *ZEPHYR IN PINSTRIPES,* FOR AN ACCOUNT OF THE YEAR CRAIGY AND ARNIE BECAME FRIENDS.}

POSITIVE, SOCIAL, AGREEMENT # 22

I WILL be actively curious about people who look, believe and behave differently from myself (using care and common sense) and seek to understand them

RATHER THAN sensing their difference(s), coming to fear, isolate, or punish them because of their difference(s).

Topic Twenty-three:
Remaining open to new experiences and beliefs

AGE 9 ½ [GRADE NINE]

DI - I ADMIRE MOM AND POP MORE THAN ANYBODY, AND ONE OF THE THINGS I ADMIRE THE MOST IS HOW OPEN THEY ARE TO NEW IDEAS AND HOW IMPORTANT IT IS TO THEM TO KEEP LEARNING NEW THINGS. EVERY SEMESTER POP READS ALL MY SCHOOL BOOKS FROM COVER TO COVER AND I IMAGINE HE'D MAKE BETTER THAN JUST A PASSING GRADE ON THE TESTS. OCCASIONALLY MOM WILL READ IN THEM BUT SHE'S MORE INTO BOOKS FROM THE LIBRARY. POP DROPPED OUT OF SCHOOL WHEN HE WAS IN THE 4TH GRADE - THAT'S MY AGE RIGHT NOW - SO HE COULD WORK TO SUPPORT HIS FAMILY. MOM FINISHED 9TH GRADE - THE GRADE I'M IN RIGHT NOW. IN BOTH CASES IT WAS THE HIGHEST GRADE ANYONE IN THEIR FAMILIES HAD EVER ACHIEVED. WHEN I GET AN IDEA, POP NEVER SAYS "NO" TO BEGIN WITH - HE SAYS, "SHOW ME." - SHOW ME THE EVIDENCE OR SHOW ME THE INFORMATION OR SHOW ME JUST HOW YOU ARE GOING TO DO IT, AND SO ON. HE'S OPEN TO NEW THINGS AND I THINK THAT'S WONDERFUL. LOTS OF PEOPLE AREN'T - LIKE MISS BARRY FOR EXAMPLE. SHE HASN'T CONTEMPLATED A NEW IDEA SINCE SHE BEGAN TEACHING 30 YEARS AGO. PARSON TENDS TO BE THAT WAY WHEN IT COMES TO RELIGION BUT HE IS SURPRISINGLY OPEN IN OTHER AREAS - LIKE THE SKYLIGHT I DESIGNED FOR HIS OFFICE TO SAVE ON ELECTRICITY AND COVERING THE CLANGER ON THE BELL WITH RUBBER FROM INNER TUBES SO IT WOULD PRODUCE A MELLOW, LESS ABRASIVE SOUND. (EVERYBODY IN TOWN USED TO COMPLAIN ABOUT IT - NOW THEY LOVE IT.) PEOPLE WHO REMAIN STUCK WITH ONLY THE OLD IDEAS NEVER GROW, NEVER FIND BETTER WAYS. I PERSONALLY TRY NEW WAYS ALL THE TIME. LOTS OF THEM DON'T WORK VERY WELL SO I GIVE THEM UP OR CHANGE

THEM BUT IF I'D NEVER INVESTIGATED THEM IN THE FIRST PLACE, LOOK AT ALL I'D HAVE MISSED. MR. GOLDSMITH CAUTIONS ME NOT TO THROW OUT THE OLD WAYS JUST BECAUSE THEY ARE OLD. LOTS OF OLD WAYS POSSESS THE WISDOM OF THE AGES - TRIED AND TRUE YOU MIGHT SAY. I THINK THAT COMES STRAIGHT FROM HIS JEWISH BACKGROUND - JEWS SEEM TO TREASURE THEIR TRADITIONS MORE THAN THE REST OF US. I HOPE I HAVE SOME TRADITIONS TO TREASURE SOME DAY. I LIKE TALKING WITH THEM (THE GOLDSMITHS, NOT TRADITIONS - THOUGH THE OTHER WOULD BE MOST FASCINATING IF I COULD DO IT) AND I TRY TO DROP IN FOR BREAKFAST AT LEAST ONCE A WEEK. THEY EAT AT 6:45 LIKE CLOCKWORK. I THINK A SCHEDULE GIVES THEM A SENSE OF SECURITY (THE GOLDSMITHS NOT JEWS IN GENERAL). I WONDER HOW I'D BELIEVE ABOUT THINGS NOW IF I'D BEEN RAISED A JEW INSTEAD OF A BLACK FUNDAMENTALIST PROTESTANT? (NOT MANY AGNOSTIC, CAUCASIAN, LADS CAN SAY THAT! HA! HA!) DIFFERENTLY, I'M SURE. I WONDER HOW I'D BELIEVE IF I'D BEEN RAISED BY MY NATURAL PARENTS. I USED TO WORRY ABOUT GROWING UP DIFFERENTLY FROM HOW THEY WOULD WANT FOR ME TO BE, BUT PARSON SAID THEY WERE GOOD PEOPLE AND WOULD WANT ME TO GROW UP THOUGHTFULLY AND BECOME MY OWN PERSON. THAT WAS VERY GOOD ADVICE - AT LEAST IT PUT AN END TO MY WORRYING. I GET TICKLED (AND A BIT IRRITATED, I MUST ADMIT) AT RELIGIOUS LEADERS IN PARTICULAR - PREACHING HOW THEIRS IS THE ONE TRUE RELIGION. DO THEY NEVER STOP TO THINK THAT IF THEY HAD BEEN RAISED IN A VERY DIFFERENT CULTURE THEY WOULD UNDOUBTEDLY BE PREACHING THAT OTHER WAY WAS THE ONE TRUE WAY? I ASKED PARSON THAT VERY QUESTION ONCE. HIS RESPONSE SHOULD NOT HAVE SURPRISED ME. HE AGREED THAT, YES, THAT WOULD BE TRUE AND THAT WAS WHY HE WAS SO THANKFUL THAT HE HAD BEEN FORTUNATE ENOUGH TO BE BORN INTO THE ONE TRULY

RIGHT RELIGION. AT FIRST, I THOUGHT HE WAS ACTUALLY TRYING TO MAKE A JOKE. THEN I SAW HE WAS SERIOUS. HOW CAN SUCH A SMART MAN MISS THE WHOLE POINT SO COMPLETELY????? (AND APPARENTLY SO EASILY!!!!)

POSITIVE, SOCIAL, AGREEMENT # 23

I WILL remain open to new experiences and beliefs and will evaluate their positive worth, absorbing or adapting those that will enhance my (our) ability to improve the human condition,

RATHER THAN remain closed to the new and different to merely protect the status quo

BECAUSE perfecting society and the human condition must be an ongoing, evolving process rather than a single state to be achieved and never modified. I will think in terms of *perfecting* rather than of *perfection*.

Topic Twenty-four:
Accepting the unknown merely as the unknown

AGE 8 ½ [GRADE SEVEN]
DEAR DI,
    I GOT SENT OUT OF SUNDAY SCHOOL AGAIN TODAY. (THAT SOUNDS LIKE IT WAS TWICE TODAY BUT I MEANT, " AGAIN TODAY, I GOT SENT OUT OF SUNDAY SCHOOL.") I HAVE FOUND IT IS HARD TO TRY AND FIT LOGIC AND SCIENTIFIC FINDINGS INTO RELIGIOUS DISCUSSIONS. SUNDAY SCHOOL TEACHERS SEEM TO HATE BEING ASKED HOW THEY KNOW FOR SURE WHAT THEY ARE TEACHING IS REALLY THE TRUTH. I USUALLY GET SOMETHING LIKE, "GOD SAYS IT'S THAT WAY." THEN I ASK, "HOW DO YOU KNOW GOD SAYS THAT?" THEN THEY SAY, "IT'S IN THE BIBLE." I SAY, "NO IT ISN'T. I'VE READ THE BIBLE AND IT DOES NOT SAY THAT ANYWHERE." THEN I GET SENT OUT OF CLASS. I DOUBT IF SHE'S LYING ABOUT IT - INTENTIONALLY. I GUESS SS TEACHERS ARE ILL PREPARED - JUST PRETTY IGNORANT OF THE FACTS. THEY DO TEND TO EXPLAIN ANYTHING THAT HAS NO SCIENTIFIC ANSWERS BY REFERRING TO, "GOD SAYS SO." SINCE SS TEACHERS ARE GENERALLY PRETTY GOOD FOLKS, I HAVE TO ASSUME THEY ARE AFRAID TO JUST SAY, "I DON'T KNOW" OR "I DON'T HAVE A REALLY GOOD ANSWER FOR YOUR QUESTION." I PERSONALLY PREFER TO JUST LEAVE THINGS AS "ANSWER UNKNOWN" INSTEAD OF MAKING UP STORIES TO EXPLAIN SOMETHING. IT MIXES FACTS AND OPINIONS TOGETHER AND IT MAKES IT PRETTY HARD TO SEPARATE WHAT IS ACTUAL FROM WHAT ARE FAIRYTALES. I'M NOT SURE SS IS SUCH A USEFUL EXPERIENCE FOR ME (ALTHOUGH I THINK IT COULD BE GOOD FOR THE SS TEACHERS IF THEY'D JUST LISTEN TO ME). I'LL DISCUSS IT WITH PARSON.

AGE 9 [GRADE NINE]
DEAR DI -
    YOU KNOW ABOUT THE RUN DOWN OLD HOUSTON HOUSE OUT ON THE FAR WEST END OF THE HILL. EVERYBODY KNOWS THAT IF YOU'RE IN THE SECOND CROTCH OF THE ELM TREE RIGHT AFTER DARK THAT THE WINDOWS IN THE CUPOLA LIGHT UP SEVERAL NIGHTS A MONTH. THE STORY AMONG THE KIDS IS THAT OLD MRS. HOUSTON LIGHTS A CANDLE UP THERE SO HER DEAD HUSBAND CAN FIND HIS WAY HOME. ONE PROBLEM - MRS. HOUSTON HAS BEEN DEAD FOR 30 YEARS, HERSELF. JOHN AND BILLY AND I WERE UP THERE TONIGHT AND WE SAW IT PLAIN AS DAY - (BAD ANALOGY) PLAIN AS COULD BE. WHEN I TOLD THE GUYS EXACTLY WHEN THE LIGHT WOULD COME ON AND THEN EXACTLY WHEN IT WOULD GO OFF THEY DECIDED I WAS IN LEAGUE WITH THE DEVIL. EVERY GENERATION OF BOYS FOR 30 YEARS HAS KNOWN IT WAS MRS. HOUSTON'S GHOST LIGHTING A CANDLE. I'M NOT SURE IF IT'S RIGHT FOR ME TO TELL THEM HOW IT REALLY HAPPENS. NONE OF THE ADULTS AROUND HERE SEEM TO KNOW EITHER. IT IS ALL JUST ANOTHER OF THOSE 'UNABLE TO STAND SOMETHING BEING UNEXPLAINED' THINGS SO AN ANSWER GETS FABRICATED. I NEVER BOUGHT THE STORY, OF COURSE - NOT BEING COMPLETELY SOLD YET ON THE SPIRIT WORLD - BUT THEN I DIDN'T HAVE AN ANSWER EITHER. I JUST PUT IT IN THE CATEGORY OF "UNKNOWN PHENOMENA" AND THAT WAS FINE. OTHER KIDS CAN'T SEEM TO DO THAT. (NEITHER CAN BILLY'S MOM. SHE STILL BELIEVES THE GHOST STORY. I IMAGINE LOTS OF OTHER GROWNUPS AROUND HERE DO, TOO.) WELL, I'LL TELL <u>YOU</u>, DI. I DON'T KNOW IF I'LL TELL THE GUYS OR NOT, THOUGH. IT'S LIKE A RITE OF PASSAGE AROUND HERE FOR BOYS TO SIT IN THAT TREE WAITING FOR THE GHOST LADY TO DO HER THING. IT'S LIKE A WAY TO PROVE HOW BRAVE YOU ARE AT EIGHT OR NINE OR SO. FIRST, IT ONLY HAPPENS 2 OR 3 NIGHTS A MONTH AT VARYING TIMES FROM MONTH TO MONTH. IT'S

WHEN THE MOON IS FULL WHICH THE KIDS THINK HELPS PROVE IT IS SUPERNATURAL. I WAS UP THERE EVERY NIGHT LAST MONTH AND I COULD MAKE IT APPEAR NINE NIGHTS IN A ROW - BUT I HAD TO MOVE FROM TREE TO TREE GOING EAST TO ACCOMPLISH THAT. YOU SEE, DI, IT'S THE WAY THE MOONLIGHT REFLECTS OFF THE WINDOW. TONIGHT, I WATCHED THE "MOON SHADOW" MOVING ACROSS THE HILLSIDE SO I KNEW WHEN IT WAS ABOUT TO HIT THE WINDOW AND THEN AGAIN WHEN IT WAS ABOUT TO MOVE ON. SO, NOW, I CAN MOVE THAT GHOST STORY OUT OF THE "ANSWER UNKNOWN" CATEGORY AND INTO THE "SATISFACTORILY ANSWERED" CATEGORY. I THINK I'LL JUST KEEP THE REAL REASON TO MYSELF - UNLESS I SHOULD HAVE TO DEFEND MYSELF AT CHURCH AGAINST BEING THE DEVIL'S HELPER. (THE DEVIL! NOW THERE'S ANOTHER OPINION-LACED UNKNOWN.)

POSITIVE, SOCIAL, AGREEMENT # 24

I WILL accept the fact that there are no ready and reasonable answers or explanations for certain aspects of life, living and processes of the universe, and view those unknowns as "current givens" and opportunities for future growth

RATHER THAN merely accepting or formulating fanciful stories, that "explain" them (or, if I do decide to live according to such lore, I will be mindful that it is *opinion,* which I have chose to follow or believe, rather than *fact* – in the usual sense of the word).

SECTION FOUR

My Final Thoughts
(Well, temporarily final, at least !)

Fifty-five years later, I am still pursuing Craigy's 'month long' campaign to save the World. In the main, I remain more challenged than disillusioned.

Here are several things I still want to believe about human beings (although I must admit that, from time to time, I have had to question them, given the continuing sad state of our World Society).

1. That we are not so innately selfish that we require the ever-present image of a punishing god (or Santa Clause) who will send us to eternal damnation (or withhold goodies) if we aren't nice people. (Or, more positively, that we are good people, because that is human nature and that it only makes good, long-term sense to be good people.)

2. That we are (or can become), as a species, ultimately concerned about the welfare of all human beings now and in the future, and are willing to regularly and altruistically demonstrate that.

3. That improving the universal human condition can become more important to human beings than the accumulation of money, stuff and power. [More on this topic in Appendix Two, *Building A User-Friendly Society*.]

4. That we are willing to take the time necessary to think through our social and personal relationships so they turn out well for all concerned each time we encounter a fellow human being.

5. That we will not allow ourselves to remain ignorant once we understand there are good, reasonable and proven answers or procedures available.

6. That as parents (and as adults, in general) we accept the "agreements" (in one form or another) and are committed to regularly modeling them for all children.

7. That life-affirming *love*, lived and administered rationally, is far more reasonable, powerful and helpful than *hate* – the ultimate and inevitable annihilator – in any of its several forms.

I had a teacher in High School who, although I disliked her general approach to living because she ignored all facts not in agreement with her own viewpoint, did leave one indelible, positive, impression on me. When class was over, she would always say, "Do right, now, you hear!"

Perhaps, saving the World (Humanity) really does just boil down to Craigy's very early and perhaps not so naive observation. "Just be nice!"

So, I leave you with this final thought: *Do right! Be nice! And build a wonderfully nurturing life for yourself and those you are privileged to touch.*

APPENDIX ONE

The Johnny Appleseed of Smiles
by Gary Hutchison

(A true-life odyssey of personal discovery by a five year old boy,
suddenly possessed with magical personal powers!)

[Originally titled: *The Positive Social Encounter*]
(C) 1961, 1996, and, 2002 by Gary Hutchison, USA
All rights reserved.

When I was five years old, I discovered something truly remarkable about myself. I possessed absolutely awesome magical powers! It's true!! By merely smiling at Grumpy old Mr. Graves, I could transform his mean looking, perennially scary face, into a happy, grinning, pleasure center.

It gets even better! When I would sidle up beside him and begin talking, grumpy old Mr. Graves would speak back to me, and, I observed, in a most pleasant tone and manner.

Well, every kid in town knew that grumpy old Mr. Graves had never smiled in his entire long, long, life, and that he only spoke when absolutely necessary - like when ordering things in stores and such. So, you can understand how I, and all of my friends, were fully convinced that I possessed magnificent magical powers, never before known in the entire history of man. Having been an orphan, I fantasized about the possibility that I had, in reality, come from another planet - Grinton, perhaps - having been sent to Earth to save mankind.

Buddy, the one, nay-saying, disbeliever in the group, bet me my powers weren't strong enough to get a smile out of Miss Terry (Miss Terry the Terrible, as she was known). She had taught 8th grade math since time began - or so the story went. A rare, breath-holding hush fell over that gathering of my devoted, fellow, pre-school followers, as, chin up, I fearlessly accepted Buddy's challenge.

It was widely accepted among the younger set in those parts, that Miss Terry's cheeks had been formed without the necessary muscles required to pull them into a smile. It was also common knowledge that her heart had been formed from a lump of blackest coal, thereby explaining why she possessed no feelings of kindness, whatsoever!

I had my job cut out for me - no doubt about that!

Push came to shove one cold February morning at precisely seven thirty five, as Miss Terry predictably left her home for the walk to school. With four witnesses hiding in the shrubs that lined the sidewalk, I met her at her gate. I opened it for her saying, "Good morning, Miss Terry," in as cheery a voice and with as smiley a face as I could muster, considering the significant distraction of my chest busting, run-away, thumping heart.

:"Well, Good morning to you, Master Craigy and thank you so much for opening the gate. You're becoming quite the young gentleman."

There was a smile on her face. Perhaps just a hint, but I had seen a smile. Both corners of her mouth turned up and that certainly qualified as a smile, even if it had lasted but a second. I sure hoped that at least one of the other guys had been close enough to verify it!

Apparently my young compatriots were less well hidden than they should have been, for as she passed each one, she nodded her head, again smiled that fleeting smile, and - by name - bade them each, "Good morning."

From that day forward, I proudly carried the nickname, "Ol'

M-1," (the Magic One).

That night it came to me, that not only had I caused her to smile and be pleasant to me, I had also, passed on the urge for her to pleasantly greet others she would meet that day! An overwhelming feeling of absolute power surged throughout my young being.

In the weeks following the discovery of my awesome, new found powers, I contemplated, all quite seriously, how I should use them. I considered several marvelous secret identities ("Smileman," and "The Grinning Guy"), complete with cape, cowl and coral tights, but, seeing as my friends already knew about my powers, I decided there would really be no way to keep secret, even such a fine alter ego.

My own hero, at five (and in some ways, even today, I suppose), was Johnny Appleseed. His unselfish seeding of the Midwestern United States with fruit to feed a generation that he would never even know, had made a tremendous impact on me. In my home, an altruistic approach to living was the cornerstone of our value system, also, and had been thoughtfully imparted to me even by that early age.

I remember - as if it were yesterday - that April morning when I awoke at daybreak, sat up straight in my bed and said out loud: "I'll become the Johnny Appleseed of Smiles."

I scrambled into my pin striped coverhalls (as I called them), sped down stairs, and stopped off in Mom and Pop's bedroom only long enough to solemnly take my mother's hand in mine and make this earnest request: "From now on, Mom, please call me Johnny."

Then, off I put to begin my mission in life, and may I just add, it has been a grand and rewarding mission (even - alas - without the snazzy, corral, tights!).

By age six I noticed that my friends would often get the same pleasant looks and cheery conversation from those at whom they would flash a smile. Rather than being in any way disheartened by their parallel success, I just figured that somehow I had been able to mystically impart some small portion of my magic to them. What a powerfully helpful guy I was becoming! I knew my parents were proud of me for it, even though, for some unexplainable reason, they opted to continue calling me Craigy.

As a child I didn't, of course, understand the psychological principles behind my 'powers,' though I did pretty accurately comprehend the sociological impact. Treat people - even total strangers - with kindness and respect, and most will immediately be affected in two major, positive ways:
First, they will relax and acquire a reassuring sense of personal safety and trust as they are reminded that there truly are friendly and comfortable people out there in their World.
Second, except for the most shy or vilest of the lot, they tend to pass on that pleasant, reassuring, experience - that *Positive Social Encounter* - to at least the next several people they, themselves, meet.

This ripple effect is unbelievable. At seven I had calculated that if I performed my magic on just two people early each morning, and each of them did the same with only two others and so on down the line - repeated just nine more times - that by nine A.M., over one thousand folks would have been *"smilized"* (as I had come to call the process). Considering that there were only 407 people in my little town, (well, 406 if you read the sign on the north end of town) that meant that quite a few got a double dose, which seemed all quite fitting, considering the generalized early morning grumpiness I had encountered on the west side of town. I always tried to smilize Mr. Miller, the rural mailman, before he began his five A.M. route. That way, I assumed, he could smilize the entire surrounding country-side.

Presently, I noticed a new aspect to this whole smilizing thing: My mere presence (even without a smile on my face or a cheery greeting from my mouth) brought out smiles and happy conversation from most all of those I'd meet. The grown-ups would all grin in my direction, chat with me a while, and pat me on my head. Wow! That seemed to prove it, all right. I could even smile telepathically!! What a revelation!

Now, you may not care to understand anymore about smilizing than I did at age six, and that's fine. Just smile your way through the byways of your life, offer pleasant greetings to those you meet, and manage a simple friendly nod to those who are beyond earshot. You will become a major and important player in smilizing the faces and warming the hearts of all America (and beyond!). (You see I've recently discovered that I can now transfer my magical powers to others by merely writing things for them to read. Will wonders never cease!!!)

If, however, you care to pursue the philosophical, sociological, and psychological aspects of the process, read on.

The basic social / psychological fact of the matter is this: A World or neighborhood or household, populated by unhappy, discontent, suspicious or angry people, is an uncomfortable, if not an outright frightening and hurtful place in which to live. When populated by happy, helpful, content, trusting, and caring people, life can be grand!

The basic philosophic premise is this: Whether motivated by an altruistic desire to improve the lot of all mankind; or merely by the more self-centered desire to live a comfortable life, unhassled by angry, maladjusted people, and to be freed from the significant dollar costs stemming from mental illness, crime and such; helping the people of the World to become happier and better adjusted, greatly eases and improves your own, and everyone else's, state of affairs. Not to do so, inevitability hurts everyone, including yourself, and just may eventually cause the destruction of the human species.

The basic method is this - the *Positive Social Encounter*: People who practice P.S.E. – at home, socially and in business - thoughtfully attempt to make each encounter with another person, a positive, comfortable, self-esteem providing, experience. We want that other person to leave us feeling good about us, himself, and the nature of the population in general. This builds a sense of trust, belonging, acceptance, importance, and ultimately, allows a secure and caring relationship within the family of man. People who feel that way are quite likely to become positive, contributing, pleasant, easy to get along with folks! What a grand World that will be!!

No one dares be too busy for this simple, gentle activity. How much extra time does it take to smile or nod or say, "Good morning," as you pass someone on the sidewalk or in the hall? None, of course. It's not an undertaking that can be fully successful when practiced by only a few - though every practitioner helps. So, let us make it a point to smile, nod, chat, listen, support, please and thank you, our ways through each encounter, every day. Mankind will be glad you did. You will be glad you did. There is no finer, spirit cleansing, feeling than to lie in bed at night knowing that because of your own positive efforts during the day just past, the World is a better, happier, place than you had found it that morning.

Recently, and partly due, I suppose to the fact my hair is now white and my walk has slowed a bit, I have discovered an interesting twist to the whole smilizing process. For most of my life, when someone in a car, and I on foot, would approach an intersection simultaneously, even though I had the right of way, I would smile, wave, and motion the car to go ahead of me. Most drivers smiled back and I assume they got my message that there truly were some nice guys left in their World (at worst, I had given them no reason to be angered by being slowed on their way to some place important to them).

These days, I often assert my right and move out into the intersection, but as I get to the mid-way point, I always turn and wave at the driver, mouthing a big, "Thank you." My theory is this: Before, when I merely motioned them on, they realized that I was a good guy. Now, from my, 'thank you,' to them, they not only know I'm a good guy, but by letting me go first, they also understand that THEY are a good guy. And how will folks who see themselves as good guys act toward others they are about to meet? Perhaps all these years I have been missing the very best aspect of this smilizing process. I'm pleased I finally slowed down enough to discover it! We must each believe we're a good guy!

End note: The old brain - that part of our brain that we humans share with the lower animals - allows us to become selfishly angry and vengeful in order to survive in the kill or be killed world of the wolves, sharks and tigers. The new brain, possessed by us humans, allows us to easily skip right over those primitive angry and revenge reactions, and, instead, act as the calm, rational, logical, helpful, caring, beings, only we humans, in all of the known universe, can be. To do less, renounces and abandons our humanity, and lowers us to the level of .... I believe that along with this magnificent, fleeting, privilege to be this human being that we are, comes the responsibility to utilize those absolutely unique, higher plane powers that have been passed on to us, alone.

If you are prone to exhibit those lower level responses of anger, rage, and revenge, take time and learn how to use the new - the exclusively human - part of your brain instead. There are a wide variety of counselors available to assist you. Chances are that it is not even your doing that you were taught to respond with that automatic, self-centered, old-brain-anger, but now its time to grow up and replace those primitive patterns with the more positive, helpful, growth-producing, human-like traits. [See my book, *Deep Mind Mastery*, if you are sincerely interested in learning more.]

Your approach to living can be that of a careful problem solver: calm, happy, comfortable, rational, caring and rewarding. It need not focus on those self-defeating, unproductive, angry, vengeful feelings, or on the personal unfairness often read into certain situations. Every heart-launched smile brings you one step closer.

My wish for you is an actively positive approach to living your life, so that you, and those around you, can each experience a comfortable, helpful, happy, fruitful life - the most precious birthright of every *human* being.

APPENDIX TWO:
Designing a *User Friendly* Society
by
Gary Hutchison

(C) 1986, 2002 U.S.A., by Gary Hutchison, All rights reserved.
[From the keynote address given to the
Fifth Annual Symposium on Human Survival,
Washington, DC, 8/8/86]

I once posed this problem to a college philosophy class: "If you were king of the World, and it was your sincere goal to build a completely peaceful, people-friendly planet, what *one* thing would you do to insure it?" A pre-ministerial student eagerly raised his hand. "I'd use everything in my power to force everyone to become pacifists." The class giggled, understanding that since pacifists hold that any kind of violence - 'force' - is wrong, his solution had a major, built in, modeling problem on the part of the king.

However, approached in a more gentle, *before* the fact manner, rather than from his confrontational, forceful, *after*-the-fact manner, it might, indeed, have some merit. Foster in the children - through adult modeling - personalities that cherish and practice peaceful problem solving, a willing mutual helpfulness, and a sense that all life is precious, and the deed just might get done.

There is a point of view, apparent throughout the pages of history, that provides the skeleton for such a plan. I have come to call its two facets by the names, *Reciprocal Esteem* and *Mutual Facilitation*. Most simply it may stated this way: *We all respect one another's basic human rights, and always only do to and for each other those things that we <u>thoughtfully</u> believe will be best for <u>all</u> concerned in the long run.* The first half defines Reciprocal Esteem; the last half, Mutual Facilitation. (Let us set aside for the moment the remaining problem of agreeing on the definition of the terms "basic human rights" and "best"!)

This approach to living is actually practiced quite regularly and successfully in many homes and communes, and to some extent in certain small neighborhoods. It has never been very successful much beyond that range, however. Why not? Doesn't it make sense that a World filled with well cared for - that is happy, content, trustworthy, caring, productive, helpful - people, would be a pretty ideal place in which to live? Doesn't it also make sense that a World populated with the opposite - sad, untrusting, deceitful, hurtful, vengeful people - would be a pretty terrifying and stifling place in which to live? And yet, how often, down through history, has mankind apparently opted to live in this *second* way? Almost always!

Why? There may be no one easy answer, and then again, perhaps there is. The history books I've read, have quite clearly pointed out to me that every time man chooses to live by *competition* rather than by *cooperation*, society disintegrates, becoming a disagreeable, hurtful, fearsome place in which to live. On the one end there develops a very small, very powerful, very rich and very self-centered "upper" class. On the other end, a very large, very helpless, very poor, very angry and vengeful "lower" class develops. The day always finally arrives when the discontented, angry, poor guys overthrow the contented, self-absorbed, rich guys, and the process begins all over again. It is the progression of most major societies down through history.

And why do so many people seem so bent on becoming

wealthy and powerful, and lording it over those who are not? Mainly, I believe, because they have been misled into believing that having lots of stuff and lots of control, are the dual secrets to happiness. I believe that is the biggest, ugliest, most disastrous, deception in human history.

Happiness has nothing to do with the acquisition of either of those things. Happiness is strictly a matter of constructing a set of positive values that move the human species on toward its ultimate positive development, and, then, living by those values day in and day out. (More simply: Continually trying your best to do good things for, and to do right by, your neighbors.)

To do this brings a *sense of integrity*, and integrity is the only source of true, deep down, forever and ever inner happiness! There is no finer, spirit cleansing, feeling, than to lie in bed at night knowing that because of your own positive efforts during the day just past, the World is a better, gentler, happier, place than you had found it that morning.

Read the history books. It's all there. And yet, generation after generation we insist on reinventing the happiness wheel all over again. And generation after generation we insist on building it all wrong. It's as if our necessarily vigilant and combative Cave Man brain - which served us well as we competed with the lower animals for survival - is still in charge of our social expectations.

Not everyone builds it all wrong of course. Many families produce children who do have a realistic, positive perspective about the human social process. Others, sadly, do not.

It has been my observation that people come in four general types, relative to all of this.

One is the *User*. The *User* takes advantage of others, using them in whatever ways fit his selfish purposes, and without regard to the welfare of that other person.

The *Observer* is a person who just sits on the sidelines of life, watching it pass by but without ever jumping in and getting involved or making a difference. Although he may never actually do specific harm to anyone, he most certainly makes no useful contribution to society. In some ways, his *inaction* may well be harmful, as he fails to support educational, charitable, political, or research efforts that could benefit himself and the rest of us.

A third approach is that of the *Destroyer*, who takes what he wants regardless of who or what gets hurt, damaged or eliminated in the process. As is obvious, none of these three categories is helpful for the survival of the human species, nor to the improvement of society. Instead, each one damages and consumes society.

The fourth category is the *Builder* - the one who uses his uniquely human talents and insights to renew, improve, and enrich society and the human species. The Builder is always the calm, systematic problem solver, and never the blamer/ hater/ punisher/ revenge taker. It is my belief, that because, as *human* beings, we have the innate positive capacity to be *Builders*, (something no other species in the entire known universe possesses), it is therefore our responsibility and *obligation* to become Builders.

Only the Builder can protect and improve the human species, and it seems important to me that we do just that. It seems to me that each person should take advantage of his or her own special talents in order to become all that he can become as a *human* being. To do less, lets *himself* down as well as *the rest of us*. It leaves him at the unfinished level of just another lower animal, willing to live in the kill or be killed realm of the lower animals.

Even when one does not feel that *he* has an *obligation* to become all that the human being - which he is - can possibly become, he probably could agree that it would be wrong to interfere with *another* human being's right to try and become as fine and complete a human being as he or she can possibly become.

I am going to suggest eight processes or values or beliefs - I call them **tenets** - which I believe will lead children (and adults) to become *Builders*, and which will keep them from getting trapped into one of the other three harmful, self destructive, less than fully human categories of personalities. These, I suggest, are *The Basic Pillars of a User Friendly Society.*

The **First** tenet states: *I cannot ask anyone else to do helpful things for me, if I am not also willing to do helpful things* *for them or others.* This is a prime characteristic of the *Builder Personality*, and is the exact opposite from the prime characteristic of the User, the Observer and the Destroyer, all three of whom always put their own, selfish interests ahead of everyone else.

Second, the Builder believes: *I have the right to my life for as long as it naturally lasts and (under most circumstances) I must grant all others this same right.* The User will protect someone's life only so long as that person is useful to him. The Destroyer sees what he wants and takes it, with no regard, for the life or well-being of anyone standing in the way. The Observer would just passively watch as someone else was being harmed.

A **Third** belief of the Builders of the World is this: *In order to have become the good person who I am today, I have needed the help of many other people along the way, so I must therefore be willing to help others as they grow and mature and search after their way.* The Users would certainly agree that they need the help of others, and constantly take advantage of others in this regard, but to then feel any obligation to be helpful in return, would make no sense to them. The Destroyers would typically feel they are self-made men, so owe no one anything. The Observer is never tuned into giving, of course, and is usually so detached from others that he receives few requests for help.

Fourth: *Since I need to be able to completely trust those around me,* (and since I am not willing to ask others to be ways for me that I am not also willing to be for them), *I must be completely trustworthy in all my interactions with others.* The whole concept of trust is virtually irrelevant to the Observer, since he avoids meaningful interaction of all kinds. The User works hard to gain your trust, so he can then take advantage of you and laugh in your face about your having been so gullible as to fall for his line. The Destroyer seldom makes any pretense of being trustworthy himself, and almost never trusts anyone else, which is how he *must* function in order to survive among his many enemies.

Fifth, the Builder fully understands that: *In order to survive emotionally and have a good life, I need approval from others, and I must therefore do my part by giving that same kind of approval to others."* Neither Users nor Destroyers approve of anyone else, and it is certainly doubtful that deep down inside, they even ever truly approve of themselves. Observers are often so lethargic that approval seems just too effort-filled and meaningless. None of these three negative personalities can ever know and understand the wonder-filled feeling of having won someone else's approval through those unique and priceless human traits of unselfish kindness, love and appreciation.

Sixth: *Since I need good friends in order to survive and to enjoy life as a well adjusted person, I also must be, and, in fact, want to be a good friend to the others in my life.* Again, due to the aloofness of the Observer, friendship is just immaterial. The User feeds on taking advantage of friendships, so, although he may appear to be quite expert at forming close personal relationships, they are always insincere and designed for his greedy benefit only. The Destroyer may engage in friendship-*like* relationships - strategic alliances would better describe them - in order to get what he wants. Destroyers never know the joys, responsibilities and privileges of true friendship.

Seventh: *Keeping those around me well adjusted will increase my chances for a happy life, and since positive strokes and tenderness are needed for good adjustment, every day I will give large doses of those things to those around me.* The Observers make no attempts to influence others in any meaningful way, so the underlying concept of this seventh tenet is meaningless to them. Users are often willing to join any cause that will promote their own personal comfort, so they will usually buy into the idea that making others better adjusted can make their own life easier. Destroyers don't buy the "helping" idea at all. When they find someone who irritates them, they just destroy them. Why mess around with rehabilitation when "*poof,*" and they're out of the way forever? After all, the Destroyer never values the lives of those who stand in his way.

And finally, the **Eighth** tenet: *I have the right and obligation to become a competent, self-fulfilled human being (a Builder), and I must grant others this same right, and encourage them in their attempts.* Users and Destroyers - not understanding about the sources of true happiness – see those of us who pursue personal excellence as total wimps, who fail to understand that the acquisition of bunches and bunches of *stuff* and the wielding of *absolute power* is all that really counts in this life. The observer, not ever getting involved in life, may know he has the *right* to improve himself, but he certainly feels no *obligation* to ever do so.

I am certain that by now you understand where I think humanity, and this precious World of ours is headed, if, generation after generation, we continue to produce Users, Destroyers and Observers instead of Builders. The *only* certain road I see to *A User Friendly Society* is through *Reciprocal Esteem* (caring about and respecting one another) and *Mutual Facilitation* (all people joined together in doing whatever it takes to provide a safe, happy, productive life for each and every human being now and for our future generations). This precludes a society principally based on interpersonal *competition.* Rather, I believe, it requires a foundation of cooperation based on the growth producing attributes of shared guardianship, mutual respect and primarily individual - not governmental - responsibility.

I am not advocating socialism which in is purer forms precludes private ownership of property and businesses. With such a way of life comes the clear danger of losing ones identity as a precious, competent, useful, beloved individual. I am advocating mutually responsible facilitation as a means of adjusting the basic, freedom-based democratic ideal which I find to be laden with tremendous possibilities for building a User Friendly Society. Perhaps it comes down to a matter of what one holds in highest esteem - the quality and well-being of human beings themselves or the proliferation of the stuff they have to play with.

As a boy I knew the process simply as neighbors eagerly and freely giving of themselves to help neighbors. I was one of the lucky children who was raised in safety, with love, trust, responsibility, and a well focused sense of how precious it is to have this fleeting privilege to be a member of this extraordinary human species - *The Family of Man.*

Other Books from
THE FAMILY OF MAN PRESS
Family Life, Parenting, Self-improvement

Trouble Proofing Kids: G. F. Hutchison, Ph. D.
A step by step, value-based training program for parents, showing how to raise or retrain children to stay out of trouble forever. In simple terms and with abundant real-life illustrations, the book presents both the necessary philosophy and developmental psychology needed to lead youngsters toward a trouble free life. A special section is included to assist adolescents wanting to trouble proof themselves. 145 pages

The ONE RULE PLAN for Family Happiness.
G. F. Hutchison, Ph. D.
A practical, easy to read and follow training manual for parents, stressing values and rule reduction. Parents are taught how to build a family life plan based on their own personal values - not those of the author. It all boils down to one simple rule that spreads the responsibility for appropriate development among all the family members. A tried and proven, very simple, everyone wins approach to improving family life. 118

The Secrets of Deep Mind Mastery. G. F. Hutchison, Ph.D.
A systematic philosophy of wellness and personal growth based in psychology, neurology, philosophy, neural-linguistics, and the wisdom of the ages. The book is a practical manual that explains and demonstrates how the mind operates, the kinds of information it requires at each of several levels and how to control the directives by which it guides the ways one thinks, acts and makes the important choices that affect each person's life. It teaches

the reader how to quickly locate, approach, and eliminate things such as fear, unhappiness, discontent, self-doubt, anger, problem producing values and other troublesome states. It teaches the student how to replace them with accurate self-knowledge, realistic self-assurance and indomitable self-esteem through the discovery, organization and utilization of ones innate, neuropsycholigical, human capacities. (New Fourth Edition)

Values and Social Issues

A Crisis of Myths: Living five years poor among the common man: G. F. Hutchison, Ph. D.
A presentation and discussion of the beliefs and mis-beliefs held by the common man as discovered and studied by the author while living as one of them and working beside them at minimal pay jobs. A frightening lack of practical knowledge and accurate information about science and the social/psychological processes has been replaced by dangerous myths, which guide their lives and way of thinking. A series of realistic suggestions are offered.

Life As Your Precious Gift. G. F. Hutchison, Ph. D.
This volume is a collection of three short books: Love's Several Faces, Getting One's Priorities in Order and A Sense of Precious.

The first explores the concept of love and suggests that the wide ranging, often indiscriminant, use of the term has rendered it confusing if not all quite meaningless. An alternative set of precise terminology is suggested to simplify conversation, sharpen our thinking, and enhance our deepest mental functioning.

The second book talks about positive values, how to discover them, set them into a meaningful hierarchy, and make sure you actually live your life according to them. It postulates that these three steps are essential for a happy, well-adjusted, humanity-friendly life.

The third work presents the belief that a sense of preciousness is an essential, basic, predisposition that everyone must possess and demonstrate in his approach to living. The author traces the downward path he sees mankind following without it, and provides numerous clear and practical suggestions for instilling it in our children.

Taken together these presentations provide a brief and simplified version of Dr. Hutchison's social philosophy - Reciprocal Esteem.

Letters to My Teenage Friends: G. F. Hutchison, Ph.D.
For more than thirty years, Dr. Hutchison has made it his practice to follow up many of the informal chats he has with young people with a letter in which he summarizes the advice or the information he provided. Sometimes he includes an article he has written on the topic. Other times, he asks questions that he thinks the young person needs to be thinking about. This is a collection of 20 letters, which he wrote to some of his teenage friends. The topics are the same topics that teens of every era have had to struggle with: love, anger, values, self-assertion, self-confidence, making your point, competition, cooperation, happiness, the future, what it means to live a good life, priorities, relationships and even some information about how the mind is structured and how knowing that can help make life go along easier

Novels for middle-grades through young adults

Secrets of the Hidden Valley: David Drake
A fantasy adventure novel for middle and upper grade readers. A twelve year old boy suddenly finds himself parentless and stranded alone in a lost valley filled with ancient American Indian

mysteries and magic. Two most unlikely companions join him. Magically transformed into Native American lads when they don their stunning buckskins, they mount their beautiful palomino ponies and race off into one "day-saving" adventure after another. The story demonstrates how positive values and dedication to helpfulness can build a happy and successful life.

Disaster at Disappearing Creek: David Drake
A novel for teenagers.
Two teenage boys, who are the worst of enemies, become trapped together in a deep, slick-walled, dark cave. The only escape is through a tiny, seemingly unreachable hole in the roof a hundred feet above. As they work toward their common goal - escape - they grow to understand and appreciate each other. The story demonstrates the growth of positive values and mutual understanding and appreciation. It becomes apparent that judging someone without getting to know him first can lead to unfortunate mis-perceptions.

Replacement Kid: David Drake
A novel for ages ten through adult.
Twelve-year old Zach is dumped, kicking and screaming, into the county orphanage one dark, cold, November night. With his mother suddenly gone, he begins testing a relationship with the wise, old, white-bearded handyman. Rocky at first, it develops into a loving friendship. Zach systematically undermines the attempts to place him into foster and adoptive homes. A final crisis, when his old friend is seriously injured near Christmas, helps the boy set his life straight. The story is fun, touching, and rewarding reading for all ages.

Children's Collection

The Remarkable Mr. Muckanstuff, Little Wheel Finds a Home, The Rainbow Princess and Little Leaf's Grand Adventure: David Drake
These short stories develop the theme that helpfulness to others has its own special, wonder-filled rewards. Children are encouraged to draw the pictures and illustrate the stories.

Romance (teen and adult)

Family Portrait: Bonnie Brewster (Jr. High through adult)
This is a story of two romances - one is that of a teenage boy and the other is that of his single mother. The youngster struggles with the mysteries and wonders of first love and the mother basks in the revelations and wonders of mature love. It is a story of contrasts and a story of similarities. Interwoven is a suspenseful series of events in which the woman's former man friend strikes out violently against her and the boy. The new family grows strong and secure through the adversity.

Biography

Teen Diaries

Growing Up Different: the intimate diaries of twin boys. (High school and adult) Tim and Tom Parks (Edited by G. F. Hutchison, Ph. D.)
This book presents the overlapping diaries of twin boys, one of whom developed into a heterosexual and the other, a homosexual. It is a unique, touching, sensitive presentation, drawn from the pages of their very personal, separately written dual diaries (from ages seven through eighteen). The brothers struggle to understand what is taking place and to find ways of dealing with the developing different paths their lives are taking. Through it all

their love for each other never wavers, though more and more, they understand each other less and less.

36 Hours to Live: the diary of a teenage suicide! (Ages 13 and older)
Craig Franklin (Edited by G. F. Hutchison, Ph. D)
In this actual diary, Craig Franklin, a very bright, very sad 16 year old boy, carefully chronicled the final 36 hours before swallowing the pills to end his life. "As depressing as the title may sound, this may well be the most positive and uplifting book teenagers or their parents could ever read." (So says Dr. Susan Crossman, Adolescent psychologist.) The diary is cradled between a forward that sensitively prepares the reader for what is to follow and a reassuring and inspiring epilogue that provides hope and purpose to guide one through life's dark and desperate moments.

Other

Zephyr In Pinstripes: the nine year old boy with the size eighteen brain -
Craig Franklin.
Nine through adult.
This is an autobiographical novel about Craigy, a boy genius, orphaned at two and raised by a remarkable elderly couple. Although race relations is an underlying theme, the focus of the book is on the year Craigy befriends Arnie, an uneducated though wise and caring mountain man. It explores the fascinating influences they have on each other. Craigy wanted most of all to be just a regular guy. "I prayed every night to wake up just average the next morning - a little taller and a whole lot dumber. It didn't happen." His time with Arnie came as close to feeling normal as the lad would ever know.

Mystery/Suspense Novels
(Adult and young adult)

The Murder No One Committed: A Raymond Masters Mystery - Garrison Flint While consulting with a noted writer as she prepares her newest book, Raymond Masters, a retired criminal investigator is confronted with her murder. The writer had been openly hated by those who worked for her and each suspect harbors more than enough motive to want her dead. The more clues he uncovers, the more obvious becomes his conclusion: "This is a murder no one committed." (He solves it, of course! Can you beat him to discovering the unusual twist this case presents?)

The Case of the Smiling Corpse: A Raymond Masters Mystery - Garrison Flint Masters is asked to assist the home town police solve the murder of a retired banker. Was it the teen age boy whose car had killed the banker's wife; the waitress at the local café with a special interest in the handyman who, it turns out, is handy with things others than tools; the sister-in-law who may inherit the victim's estate; or a hit man hired by his wife before she was killed? Initially, it looks like suicide as the body is found in a room locked from the inside with a pistol beside the body. Perhaps it was the perfect (almost) frame. The reader will have to wait until the final paragraph to hear the old inspector's solution.

A Gathering of Killers: A Raymond Masters Mystery - Garrison Flint
Inspector Masters is at it again - this time untangling the mystery of a murder in which the body was stabbed, shot, strangled, drowned, poisoned and bludgeoned. A dozen suspects at the beautiful Whispering Pines Lodge lead him on a merry chase as he systematically sorts away the innocent and
hones in on the culprit (or is it culprits?). Again, it remains until the final page to hear the old inspector's solution.

The Man Who Refused to Die: A Raymond Masters Mystery - Garrison Flint
Not even the third time was to be the charm for this murderer. A beloved, retired, dying, classical guitarist is the eventual victim. In his mansion - curiously - live his three former wives, his long time back-up guitarist with his despicable son, his distant personal assistant, the charming young chauffeur with a shady past, the cook and the mysterious stranger. There is a twist at the end unlike the readers of Raymond Masters mysteries have ever before witnessed.

Revenge of the Restless Crossbow: A Raymond Masters Mystery - Garrison Flint
Apparently of its own volition, an antique crossbow, long perched high up on the wall of the Rafferty Mansion, fires and kills one of the guests at a publisher's book launching party. The following day another member of the group is found murdered. There are a variety of suspects: three mystery writers, a universally disliked book critic, the cantankerous neighbor and his son, the wily old grounds keeper, the maid, the new assistant to Winston Rafferty (one of the writers), and a flock of pigeons. Nothing is simple this time out. The twists and turns tangle among themselves. Masters identifies the perpetrator, of course, but the reader will have to wait until the final word of the final paragraph to hear his/her name.

The Case of the Gypsy Curse: A Raymond Masters Mystery - Garrison Flint
Seven of the past nine leaders of an off-beat fraternal order in a small Wyoming town died mysterious deaths. There have been no wounds and no traces of poison. There has, however, been a long-standing Gypsy curse against the group. Natural causes? Coincidence? Curse? Masters doesn't think so. Not only, does he nail the perpetrator(s?) of these seven crimes, but he puts the screws to four more along the way.

Red Grass at Twilight: A suspense mystery: - Garrison Flint
A bright, mild-mannered, middle aged man struggles to regain his memory while being forced to evade ugly adversaries who seem determined to stop him before that can occur. Why are so many people pursuing him? He is not at all certain which side of the law his antagonists are on and that leaves his own position in doubt - good guy or bad guy? Because of that uncertainty, he can't engage the help of the police. From the opening page in which he "emerges from a dark cloud of nothingness" possessing only two bags and an all-encompassing sense of foreboding, to the final, nail-biting, terrifying scene high atop a hotel roof, the reader is kept guessing.

Fun for Senior Citizens (and those not so senior!)

In Praise of the Common Place: Grampa Gray Based on a syndicated, daily, newspaper and ezine column by "Grampa Gray" this book takes a playfully philosophic look at modern day society, compared with 'the olden days.' The author employs an interesting combination of prose and old fashioned, bumptiy, bump, bump verse. Its perspective is that of a senior citizen and was written primarily for other members of the gray-haired set (although it is appreciated by all ages). It champions old-fashioned values and pokes fun at the author's own foibles and human frailties. Grampa finds beauty and wonder in unique subjects: lint, cobwebs, housework, recycling, ants and, of course, growing old. There are a few belly laughs per book, but mostly there are chuckles, smiles, nods of understanding, and a magnificent burst of endorphins.

BOOKS IN THE LITTLE PEOPLE OF THE OZARK MOUNTAINS(tm) SERIES
(Folklore for grown-ups who still believe in the power of childhood fantasy)
by Gary Hutchison (the only known living confidant of the Little People)
Middle grades through adult

The Little People of the Ozarks(tm) are a fun loving lot, each about as tall as a grape hyacinth. Still retaining their old world brogue, they settled the Ozark Mountains hundreds of years ago, and since then have lived as two separate clans, peaceful and loving by nature, and preferring the simple and uncomplicated, candle lit life, of days gone by. They dwell contentedly in quaint and tidy hollow stump homes, and are a most cheerful, charitable people, who thoughtfully go about practicing their magic, in order to bring happier, safer, more satisfying lives to the mortals who live near by.

Book One: The Ring of The Farjumpers. Jay, a nine and a half year old mortal boy, and Twiggs, a twelve and three quarters year old Little Person, encounter each other for the first time. A wonderful friendship develops, which, along the way necessitates close scrutiny of the two cultures by the youngsters. Then, the relationship must end, and the boys struggle to deal with the impending loss. Humorous, nostalgic, philosophical, delightful, and thought provoking. You may just see yourself on every page.

Book Two: A Man of the Clan. The odyssey continues as it describes the struggles and the successes of Twiggs (the Little Person) during the first months of coping with his new responsibilities as a Man of the Clan Dewgoodabee. He finds himself in love - another set of struggles and delights. The story reminds us that growing up, though complex, need not be an unpleasant experience. A sentimental reverie of how it was and how it could be.

Book Three: The Ambassador and The Touchperson. Jay and Twiggs have their first three meetings. Hard-nosed negotiating doesn't interfere with joy-filled escapades at the swimming hole and cabin. The year culminates with "the miracle of the millennium," as Jay's Grampa characterizes it in his country newspaper. The boys learn that even a miracle, like life itself, sometimes has an unanticipated down-side which they struggle to understand and manage.

Book Four: Twiggs and Cinnamon. Twiggs and Cinnamon are wed, and deal with the usual delights and adjustments that confront all young couples. A host of new Little People are introduced as they go about caring for themselves and the Mortals in the nearby hills and valleys. Hardy portions of delightful celebrations are enjoyed and an impending catastrophe is encountered

GENERAL FICTION

CROSSROADS Gary Hutchison

A story of romance, mystery and renewal. The story is set in an around the Crossroad Café, an isolated, though friendly gathering place run by Gramps and his troubled, fourteen year old grandson, Tommy. Into this milieu, the author sets Jake, a confused and depressed old man, on a mission of revenge, and June, Tommy's tutor - a widowed, retired, teacher. Absorbing relationships develop and are explored – Jake with Tommy, Jake with June, and Jake with the emotional battle raging within him. From the outset, Jake's sole purpose in life is to find and inflict the worst imaginable punishment on the elusive teenager, David Dalton – the local boy who will not be found.

Enjoy other
FAMILY FRIENDLY
books
from
The Family of Man Press at

www.familypress.com

www.familypress.com

Mysteries, Ozark Ghost Stories, Romance, Children and Teen, Senior Citizens, More.

Also
The kids – 9 to 14 – will want to take a look at
www.tommypowers.net
for FREE POSTERS and
info about
TOMMY POWERS
the 13 year old Super Hero.

At
www.keepingamericareading.com
you can learn about our reading initiative and how you can help support our free book program for the elderly and young.

Printed in the United States
30301LVS00001B/80